Futurability

*The Age of Impotence and
the Horizon of Possibility*

Franco 'Bifo' Berardi

T0286464

VERSO
London • New York

This paperback edition first published by Verso 2019
First published by Verso 2017, 2019
© Franco Berardi 2017, 2019

The moral rights of the author have been asserted

3 5 7 9 10 8 6 4 2

Verso
UK: 6 Meard Street, London W1F 0EG
US: 20 Jay Street, Suite 1010, Brooklyn, NY 11201
versobooks.com

Verso is the imprint of New Left Books

ISBN-13: 978-1-78478-744-8
ISBN-13: 978-1-78478-746-2 (US EBK)
ISBN-13: 978-1-78478-745-5 (UK EBK)

British Library Cataloguing in Publication Data
A catalogue record for this book is available from the British Library

The Library of Congress Has Cataloged the Hardback Edition as Follows:
Names: Berardi, Franco, author.
Title: Futurability : the age of impotence and the horizon of possibility /
  Franco 'Bifo' Berardi.
Description: Brooklyn : Verso Books, 2017. | Includes bibliographical
  references and index. |
Identifiers: LCCN 2017006308 (print) | LCCN 2017020904 (ebook) | ISBN
  9781784787462 () | ISBN 9781784787431 (alk. paper)
Subjects: LCSH: Possibility. | Power (Social sciences) |
  Globalization – Political aspects. | Civilization, Modern – Philosophy.
Classification: LCC BC199.P7 (ebook) | LCC BC199.P7 B47 2017 (print) | DDC
  303.3 – dc23
LC record available at https://lccn.loc.gov/2017006308

Typeset in Fournier MT by Hewer Text UK Ltd, Edinburgh, Scotland
Printed and bound by CPI Group (UK) Ltd, Croydon, CR0 4YY

To Juha Varto, Tere Vadén, Axeli Virtanen, and Geert Lovink, albeit with a certain delay

Contents

Introduction   1

Part I. POTENCY   31

1. The Age of Impotence   33
2. Humanism, Misogyny and Late Modern Thought   57
3. The Dark Side of Desire   92

Part II. POWER   101

4. Automation and Terror   103
5. Necro-Capitalism   132
6. Money Code and Automation   148

Part III. POSSIBILITY   161

7. Conundrum   163
8. Superstition   176
9. Disentanglement   190
10. A Short History of the General Intellect   197
11. Dynamics of the General Intellect   214
12. Invention   222

Afterword: The Inconceivable   231
Notes   241

Introduction

I'm not going to write about the future, again.

I'm not going to write about no-future, either.

I'll write about the process of becoming other: vibration, selection, recombination, recomposition.

Possibility is content, potency is energy, and power is form.

I call *possibility* a content inscribed in the present constitution of the world (that is, the immanence of possibilities). Possibility is not one, it is always plural: the possibilities inscribed in the present composition of the world are not infinite, but many. The field of possibility is not infinite because the possible is limited by the inscribed impossibilities of the present. Nevertheless, it is plural, a field of bifurcations. When facing an alternative between different possibilities, the organism enters into vibration, then proceeds making a choice that corresponds to its potency.

I call *potency* the subjective energy that deploys the possibilities and actualizes them. Potency is the energy that transforms the possibilities into actualities.

I call *power* the selections (and the exclusions) that are implied in the structure of the present as a prescription: power is the selection and enforcement of one possibility among many, and simultaneously it is the exclusion (and invisibilization) of many other possibilities.

This selection can be described as gestalt (structuring form), and it acts as a paradigm. It may also be seen as a format, a model that we can implement only by complying with the code.

Possibility

In 1937 Henri Bergson published the article 'Le possible et le réel' (The Possible and the Real) in the Swedish magazine *Nordisk Tidskrift*. In this text, later included in the book *La pensée et le mouvant*, the French thinker answers the question: what is the meaning of the word 'possibility'?

> We call possible what is not impossible: obviously, this non-impossibility is the condition of its actualisation. But this possibility is not a degree of virtuality, is not ideal pre-existence . . . From this negative sense, we shift unconsciously to the positive sense of the word. In the first definition, possibility means absence of hindrance; but we are shifting now to the meaning: pre-existence in the form of an idea.[1]

'B is possible' means that B is inscribed in A and nothing is preventing B from deploying from the present condition of A. Bergson speaks of pre-existence in the form of an idea, but I don't want to use the word 'idea', preferring to say that a future state of being is possible when it is immanent or inscribed in the present constitution of the world. However, we should not forget that the present constitution of the world contains many different (conflicting) possibilities, not only one.

Extracting and implementing one of the many immanent futurabilities: this is the shift from possible to real. Futurability is a layer of possibility that may or may not develop into actuality.

Bergson writes:

> Why is the Universe ordered? How can the rule impose itself on the irregularity, how can form impose itself on matter? . . . This problem vanishes as soon as we understand that the idea of disorder has sense in the sphere of human industry, in the sphere of fabrication, not in the field of creation. Disorder is simply an order that we do not seek.

We stare at the chaotic intricacy of matter, of events, of flows, and seek for a possibility of order, a possible organization of chaotic material. We extract fragments from the magma then try to combine them, in an attempt to reverse entropy: intelligent life is this process of local, provisional reversal of entropy. Time is the dimension of decay and resistance, of dissolution and of recomposition. Time is the process of becoming other of every fragment in every other fragment, forever. Bergson defines the concept of possibility from the point of view of time: 'Why does reality unfurl? How is it not unfurled? What purpose does time serve (I speak here of real, concrete time, and not of abstract time which is merely the fourth dimension of space)? Doesn't the existence of time prove the indeterminacy of things? Isn't time this very indeterminacy?'

The old philosophy, he says, was centred on Eternity: Immutable Categories of Being, Eternal Conjunction of Thought and Idea.

> The moderns place themselves on a different ground. They do not treat time anymore as an intruder, a perturbation of Eternity. But they would like to reduce time to a mere appearance. The temporary is for them a confusion of Reason . . . Let's forget about theories, let's stick to the facts. They do not treat time anymore as an intruder, a perturbation of Eternity.

In the first place, Bergson defines the possible in a tautological way: possible is that which is not impossible. Possible is that which is not necessarily going to exist, and simultaneously is not necessarily going to be non-existing. In the second place, Bergson acknowledges this answer is an empty one; it says nothing about the content of the possibility itself. If we want to know more we have to understand what is happening in the empty space of non-impossibility and non-necessity.

Let's look at the evolution of a living organism. The field of possibility of the organism is included in its genetic code, but the code is not the history of the future. It rather opens a range of possible evolutions, and in this range many different pathways can be taken. Epigenesis (the process by which an organism develops out of its genetic code) constantly exposes the emerging organism to the environment, to the events occurring that the code cannot predict or preform. This field of possibility is not infinite, because it is limited by the genetic conditions inscribed in the code. But it is by no means reducible to merely a deterministic succession of predictable states. As the possible is plural, the environmental events in which the code develops select and shape one form among many.

Possibility is as the intensity of the tantric egg, before and during the process of differentiation: 'What Spinoza calls singular essence, it seems to me, is an intensive quality, as if each one of us were defined by a kind of complex of intensities which refers to her/his essence, and also of relations which regulate the extended parts, the extensive parts.'[2]

In *A Thousand Plateaus,* the passage from possibility to actuality is described as a shift from the intensity of the egg to the deployment of gradients of differentiation, and finally to the full deployment of the extended body.

A Body without Organs is made in such a way that it can be occupied, populated only by intensities. Only intensities pass and circulate. Still, the Body without Organs is not a scene, a place, or even a support upon which something comes to pass. It has nothing to do with phantasy, there is nothing to interpret. The BwO causes intensities to pass; it produces and distributes them in a *spatium* that is itself intensive, lacking extension. It is not space, nor is it in space; it is matter that occupies space to a given degree – to the degree corresponding to the intensities produced. It is non-stratified, unformed, intense matter, the matrix of intensity, intensity = 0; but there is nothing negative about that zero, there are no negative or opposite intensities. Matter equals energy. Production of the real as an intensive magnitude starting at zero. That is why we treat the BwO as the full egg before the extension of the organism and the organisation of the organs, before the formation of the strata; as the intense egg defined by axes and vectors, gradients and thresholds, by dynamic tendencies involving energy transformation and kinematic

movements involving group displacement, by migrations: all independent of accessory forms because the organs appear and function
here only as pure intensities. The organ changes when it crosses a
threshold, when it changes gradient. 'No organ is constant as regards
either function or position ... sex organs sprout anywhere ...
rectums open, defecate and close ... the entire organism changes
color and consistency in split-second adjustments.' Tantric egg.[3]

The tantric egg contains uncountable inter-cellular concatenations – the web of possibility. The evolution of these
concatenations from the state of virtuality to the state of
deployed organism is the space of actualization of the possible. That which I call potency is the condition for this actualization: potency enables the shift from the zero-dimension-
ality of information to the multidimensionality of the body
and of the event. Power, then, is the grid of selections that
visualizes, emphasizes and implements one plan or consistence in which a possibility deploys itself, excluding any other
possibility from the space of actualization.

The tantric egg is the magma of all possibilities, the chaotic
content looking for a shape. The general intellect is the
content, semio-capitalism is the gestalt, the generator of
coded forms: paradigmatic capture.

Power is the subjection of possible content to a generative
code.

The horizon of our time is marked by a dilemma: in the
first scenario, the general intellect will unfold and develop
according to the paradigmatic line of the semio-capitalist
code. In the second scenario, the general intellect is combined
into form according to a principle of autonomy and of non-
dogmatic and useful knowledge.

Who will decide the outcome of this dilemma?

Who will decide the actualization of one possibility or another?

This is the issue that I'll develop in the third and final part of this book.

In order to shift from virtuality to actuality, a possibility has to be embodied in a subject and this subject needs potency. How can a possibility be embodied in a subject? How can a subject have potency?

A possibility is embodied in a subject when the magma of possibility meets a concatenation that transforms the magma into intentional subjectivity.

Liberal democracy is the political concatenation that enables the subjectivation of the bourgeois class in the centuries of modernity. Communism is the concatenation that enables industrial workers to gather and fight for social rights.

What concatenation will enable the general intellect to emerge as a conscious force intended to dismantle and reprogram the world according to the concrete usefulness of knowledge?

Potency

Potency, then, is the condition that enables transformation – according to the will of a subject.

History is the space of the emergence of possibilities embodied in subjectivities endowed with potency.

Potency gives us the potential to be free and to transform the environment. On the other hand, power is the subjection of possibilities to a generative code.

Like evolution, history can also be seen as a succession of bifurcations and selections, but in the kingdom of history at each bifurcation consciousness plays a decisive role in the selection among conflicting possibilities.

In order to emerge from the chaotic vibrational dimension of possibility, a body needs potency. Potency is the energy that links a possibility inscribed in the present with its subject.

In order to turn that possibility into form, the subject with potency has to dispense with power that counters the expansion of a conflicting inscribed possibility. Contrary to the assumption of many Spinozian scholars (I'll refer particularly to Toni Negri), potency is not infinite.

In many texts, particularly in his books *The Savage Anomaly* and *Subversive Spinoza,* Negri attributes to Spinoza the idea of an infinity of potency: 'Being does not want to be subjected to a becoming that does not possess truth. Truth is said of being, truth is revolutionary, being is already revolution.'[4] This sentence sounds strangely theological, and Negri is, actually, adamant in reclaiming the absolute nature of world. 'The world is absolute. We are happily overwhelmed by this plenitude, we cannot help but associate ourselves with this abundant circularity of sense and existence . . . This point defines the second reason for Spinoza's contemporaneity. He describes the world as absolute necessity, as presence of necessity.'[5]

The definition of the world as absolute necessity is the foundation of Negri's strenuous refusal to acknowledge the limits of potency, and is also the foundation of his faith in the necessity of liberation. From an atheist point of view, I'm obliged to abandon the faith: I don't think that liberation is necessary. Liberation is a possibility, and in our time at the beginning of the twenty-first century, it seems to be an unlikely one.

Is liberation inscribed in the absolute fabric of the world? Negri answers resoundingly: yes. But this leads to a fantastic obliteration of reality, and particularly gives way to a fantastic obliteration of the contemporary life of subjectivity. Liberation is not an absolute necessity, but a possibility that needs potency in order to be actualized. And sometimes we don't have that potency.

All the rhetorical Viagra that might be provided by Negri's reading of Spinoza is pointless when it comes to the political impotence of the contemporary subjectivity. The possibilities inscribed in social life and knowledge do not find a political concatenation, and sad passions obnubilate the possible. The genesis of such sad passions has to be understood without any hysterical denial. We must look the beast in the eyes if we want to find the way out.

In the text *On Spinoza*, Deleuze writes, '*Affectus* is the continuous variation of someone's force of existing.' This variation increases or diminishes the potency of the subject: sad passions and joyful passions are to be seen as the affecters, as the cause of this increase or diminishment. 'Spinoza denounces a plot in the universe of those who are interested in affecting us with sad passions. The priest has need of the sadness of his subjects, he needs these subjects to feel themselves guilty . . . Inspiring sad passions is necessary for the exercise of power.'[6]

To hold these sad passions should not be viewed as a sort of guilt, an error that must be emendated. Sad passions are not the effect of a misunderstanding, and they cannot be cancelled by force of will or by right consideration. As Deleuze points out, sad passions are the effect of an exercise of power.

Power is the agency that reduces the field of possibility to a prescriptive order; power, therefore, is the actual source of sad passions, and their existence can be seen as an effect of the subjugation of the soul to the force of power. 'Spinoza says that evil is a bad encounter. Encountering a body which mixes badly with your own.' Bad encounters do happen, alas. Lots of them in these times. Quoting Spinoza, Negri writes:

> Blessedness is not the reward of virtue, but virtue itself, nor do we enjoy it because we restrain our lists; on the contrary, because we enjoy it, we are able to restrain them. Spinoza overturns Hegelianism before it is born with the recognition of his own logical supremacy . . . and, in the productivity of reason, he anticipates the development of history overturning, therefore, the Hegelian affirmation of philosophy as a recording of a dissected and selected event, and therefore truly posing freedom at the basis of the event and history, rooting human power absolutely on the lower, productive border of existence. There is no distinction between phenomenological *Erklarung* and metaphysical *Darstellung*.[7]

It's hard not to see the analogy between the Spinozian pantheistic vision and the pan-logistic vision of Hegel. The difference, however, is crucial: in Hegel, infinity is the energy of the spiritual becoming; in Spinoza infinity is nature, and potency is the body.

'What can a body do?' asks Spinoza, a question intended to illuminate the excessive nature of the body, not to assert its boundless potency.

However, no one has hitherto laid down the limits to the powers of the body, that is, no one has as yet been taught by experience what the body can accomplish solely by the laws of nature, in so far as she is regarded as extension . . . Again, no one knows how or by what means the mind moves the body, nor how many various degrees of motion it can impart to the body, nor how quickly it can move it.[8]

What can our body do nowadays?

What can the social body do under the present condition of separation from the automated brain?

Impotence in the issue that I will discuss in the first part of this book.

Power

At each historical bifurcation, the range of possibilities is limited by power and simultaneously opened by the emerging subjectivity. If the emerging subjectivity has potency (internal consistence and projecting energy), it can bring an invisible possibility into the space of visibility, and can give way to the actualization of that possibility.

Morphogenesis is the emergence of a new form from a vibration, from the oscillation between different evolutions of the body of possibilities. The emerging form is contained as a possibility, but we can insert automated selections in the passage from an alternative to a solution. Automation is the replacement of human acts with machines as well as the submission of cognitive activity to logical and technological chains.

This is exactly the origin of power: the insertion of automated selections into the social vibration.

Automation is programmed by the human mind according to its projects, visions, ideologies, preconceptions: the automaton replicates the embedded intention and the established form of the relation.

What is a form in relation to its content? And how does it happen that a new form can emerge? How do things generate things, and concepts generate concepts? And finally, more interesting: how do concepts generate things?

Power can be defined as a form of engendered determinism.

In fact, power takes the form of techno-linguistic automatisms shaping future behaviour: 'If you don't pay the rent, you'll be automatically evicted from your apartment', 'If you don't pay the fee, you'll be automatically expelled from the university', and so on. The execution of the eviction or the expulsion is not the act of a human agent that might be moved by compassion and change her mind. These consequences are implicit in the technical machine, as if they were logico-mathematical necessities. They are not, but the linguistic machine records behaviour and translates it into consequences: real events are activators of mathematical functions inscribed in the machine as logical necessities.

Pre-emption prescribes in a deterministic way the future form of the organism by the insertion of biotechnical or techno-social mutations. Determinism is not only a (bad) philosophical methodology that describes the evolution in terms of causal implications, it is also a political strategy that aims to introduce causal chains in the world, and particularly in the social organism.

The determinist strategy aims to subjugate the future, to constrain tendency into a prescribed pre-emptive model, and automate future behaviour.

The effect produced by the chain of automatisms may be defined as a deterministic trap, a trap in which the possible is captured and reduced to mere probability, and the probable is enforced as necessary.

This is the issue I will discuss in the second part of this book.

Immanence Tendency and Paradigm

Immanence is the quality of being inside the process, the intrinsicality or inherence of something to something.

This book is about futurability, the multiplicity of immanent possible futures: becoming other which is already inscribed in the present.

But if we assume that the future is necessarily inscribed in the present constitution of the world, we attribute a teleological meaning to the immanence, and inscription is turned into *pre*scription.

Teleology can be based on a deterministic interpretation of scientific causation, or a theological design of the history of the world that can be labelled pantheism: God is an immanent Prescriptor.

A materialistic vision of immanence, on the contrary, is based on the persuasion that the present reality contains the future as a wide range of possibilities, and the selection of one possibility among many is not prescribed in a deterministic way in the process of morphogenesis. The future is inscribed in the present as a tendency that we can imagine: a sort of premonition, a vibrational movement of particles that are taken in an uncertain process of continuous recombination.

Immanence does not imply a logical, necessary consequentiality: the present does not contain the future as a necessary linear deployment or consequential elaboration of implications that we can read in the current reality. Immanence means all the uncountable divergent and conflicting possibilities are inscribed in the present. The present state of the world can be described as the vibrational concurrence of many possibilities. How can chaotic vibration give birth to a particular event? How does it happen that among many possibilities of development, just one of them prevails?

The future states of the social world are not the linear effect of political will, but the result of infinitely complex relations and conflicts and mediations. We call a heterogony (heterogenesis) of the ends the asymmetrical relation between projects and realizations, between will and historical composition of infinite concurring wills in the determination of an event.

The relation between now and tomorrow, between the present state of the world and the future state of the world is not necessary (that is, necessitated). The present does not contain the future as a linear development. The emergence of a form among many possible forms is the – provisional and unstable – effect of a polarization, the fixation of a pattern.

Tendency is movement in a given direction. The vibrational complexity of the world as potentiality can be interpreted in terms of coexisting and conflicting tendencies. Tendency is the possibility that seems to prevail at a given moment of the vibrational process that gives birth to the event.

At the highpoint of industrial modernity, the emancipation of social activity from salaried work was inscribed in the social concatenation, and particularly in the relation between the potency of the general intellect and the existing technology. The emancipation of human activity from capitalist exploitation was a possibility that could be viewed as a tendency. Communism was immanent in the technical composition of capital and also in the social consciousness.

Nevertheless, as we know, this possibility did not deploy into reality. The tendency towards the emancipation of human activity from capitalist exploitation (that I call 'possible communism') did not prevail.

The possibility of communism was obliterated by the event of the Bolshevik Revolution and the ensuing establishment of a dictatorship of the army and the state.

Indeed, the Leninist action broke the structural chain conceptualized by Marx. The event of the Russian Revolution, like the event of the Paris Commune, was not the necessary deployment of structural dynamics inscribed in the process of production. They were untimely events. But every event is untimely, as the event does not correspond to a chain of causation. The Russian Revolution acted as a violation or a refutation of the Marxist persuasion that socialist revolution would first begin in the most advanced industrial countries.

The event and the structure cannot be described in terms of mutual necessary implications. The structure is not necessarily implying any event, and the event is not implied in the structure.

I call paradigmatic capture the reduction of the range of possibilities inscribed in the present to a pattern that acts as a formatting gestalt.

In fact, there is a conflict between emergent possibilities and the dominant paradigm. The paradigmatic capture blocks and forbids the deployment of the tendency and stiffens the vibration reducing the multiplicity of possibilities to a new (provisional, unstable) state of the world.

We may describe the relation between society and the development of technology in terms of possibility and paradigmatic capture. Knowledge, production and technology are linked in a vibrational field of possibilities. Technology is not a chain of logical implications, but a field of immanent conflicting possibilities. Electronic technology and digital networks since the beginning of their implementation enabled a process of transformation of social relations and production, open to divergent possible evolutions.

Digital technology and research in artificial intelligence are opening the door to a sort of automation of the future.

Statisticon: Inscription Prescription

In the infinity of time, an endless chain of bifurcations gives birth to vibrations, selection, emergence. At every instant, matter enters a vibrational state, oscillating between different possibilities until a new set emerges.

The emergence of consciousness is an effect of evolution, but it is also a jump into a reflective dimension: the dimension of choice. When the time of evolution is traversed by consciousness, then we speak of history.

At this point, such bifurcations are perceived as intentional selection between possibilities.

Human beings seem to have the peculiar ability of making conscious choices and selecting one possibility among many. Conscious choices are not (only) rational processes of calculation: they imply strategic decision, ethical judgement; they express aesthetic preferences and are influenced by flows of info-psycho-stimulation.

As the future is not prescribed, and the succession of now and tomorrow is not monolithic or determined, our task consists in distinguishing the layers of futurability that lie in the texture of the present reality and in the present consciousness.

Futurability can be traced in terms of absolute necessity, relative necessity or probability, tendency, impossibility and possibility.

Absolute necessity marks the logical enunciations that are true today and will also be true tomorrow, as they are functions inscribed in the human mind and do not imply any relation with external reality.

Kant distinguishes between synthetic and analytic sentences. Analytical sentences can be considered truisms because the content of the enunciation is implied in the subject. Analytical truth is therefore a necessity.

Relative necessity, on the other hand, is a concatenation of temporal events that is likely to imply a certain probability as well as a concatenation of states of being that are enforced both by law and by force.

'If you don't pay the rent, you will be evicted' is a case of relatively necessary futurability. There is no logical necessity in the implication, but social relations are based on the enforcement of conventional rules. This enforcement may happen by force of violence, of agreement, or by force of automation.

In the computer of the real estate company, there are logical chains implying that the tenant who does not pay the rent will be expelled from the house. This implication, however, is neither logical nor natural, but is enforced by the automation of will, and by the automated transcription of a social *rapport de force*. Financial capitalism is bound up in techno-linguistic implications that pretend to be natural and logical. They are not. They are rather artificial reductions of the range of possibility to the narrow string of probability.

Pre-emption: Determinism as Strategy of Reduction

The predictive power of the contemporary global machine lies in the ability to routinely read big flows of data. The resulting statistical prediction, thanks to the introduction of the filter bubble, turns into prescription and the evacuation of subjectivity.

The techno-informational automatism that captures data from the living flow of social activity in order to adapt the articulations of the global machine to the expectations of the social organism, and in order to symmetrically adapt the expectations of the social organism to the articulations of the global machine, I'll call, following Warren Neidich, the 'Statisticon'.

The technique of customization that enables Google and other search engines to anticipate our requests, as well as to shape and control our desires, is called the 'filter bubble'. The filter bubble is an example of what Warren Neidich calls the Statisticon: a reducer of future events into probability and predictability. Pre-emption is complementary to the statistical capture; pre-emptying the future means preventing future behaviour and emptying it of singularity.

In the dynamics of the Statisticon, the mirror acts as a generator that leads the machine to anticipate and pre-package social behaviour.

The Statisticon evolves together with the environment (in this case, social life), but the condition for this coevolution is the pre-inscribed structural homology that makes social interaction possible in the sphere of automated governance.

The agent of enunciation must use the language that the machine understands, in order for there to be effective communication. Once the agent of enunciation has accepted the format that makes interaction possible, the interaction can evolve, and the machine can adapt to the living organism insofar as the living organism has also adapted to the machine.

The statistical pre-emption implies two complementary actions: one is the recording of massive flows of data; the second is the adapting of the machine to the living environment and the reciprocal adaptation of the living, conscious organisms to the machine.

Large amounts of data give the machine its ability to adapt, while simultaneously the filter bubble induces the living, conscious organisms to comply with the expected responses of the machine.

Statistical pre-emption is the mode of functioning of governance, the contemporary form of political and economic power – a form of engendered determinism.

Pre-emption acts as a deterministic trap: the future of the organism can be altered through bio-technical or techno-social modifications. The possible is captured and reduced to mere probability, and the probable is enforced as necessary.

Nevertheless at the next bifurcation a new possibility surfaces, and the next bifurcation will be the following: a process of cognitive automation underway in our time. Will the general intellect (millions of cognitarians worldwide) find a body – an erotic, aesthetic and ethical body?

Futures are inscribed in the present as immanent possibilities, not as necessary developments of a code. Futurability refers to the multidimensionality of the future: in the present a plurality of futures is inscribed. Consciousness is one of the deciding factors in the selection between these possibilities, and consciousness is continuously changing in the flow of changing social composition.

A process of cognitive automation is underway in our time. Articulations of the global machine (interfaces, applications . . .) proliferate and insert themselves in the social mind. The conjunctive body and the conjunctive mind are penetrated by the architecture of overall connectivity.

A code is inscribed in the info-neural connection; as we face this process of cognitive wiring we are often led to think that there is no way out from a sort of neurototalitarianism in the making.

A way out from neuro-totalitarianism does exist as the conjunctive body of the general intellect is wider that the code embedded in it, and the dynamics of the general intellect may lead to unexpected deviations from the determinist replication of the coded actuation.

The present depression (both psychological and economic) obscures the consciousness that no determinist projection of the future is true. We feel trapped in the tangle of techno-linguistic automatisms: finance, global competition, military escalation. But the body of the general intellect (the social and erotic bodies of a million cognitarians) is richer than the connective brain. And the present reality is richer than the format imposed on it, as the multifold possibilities inscribed in the present have not been wholly cancelled, even if they may seem presently inert.

The possible is immanent, but it's unable to develop into a process of actualization.

The inertia of the possibilities inscribed in the present composition of the social body is an effect of the impotence of subjectivity. During the last century, the social subjectivity of workers experienced forms of solidarity, autonomy and welfare – then at the end of the century it became disempowered so that it is now unable to express those potentialities which are present in the general intellect and in the body of social solidarity.

The possibility of emancipation of social time from the obligation of salaried work still exists: it is located in the cooperative knowledge of millions of cognitive workers, but this possibility cannot surface at the present because of the political impotence that in this book I want to describe, analyze and find a way to exceed.

The impotence of subjectivity is an effect of the total potency of power when it becomes independent from human will, decision and government – when it is inscribed in the automated texture of technique and of language.

Social Psycho-mancy and the Horizon of Possibility

> *The man thinks*
> *The horse thinks*
> *The sheep thinks*
> *The cow thinks*
> *The dog thinks*
> *The fish doesn't think.*
> *The fish is mute, expressionless*
> *because the fish knows.*
> *Everything.*
>
> Iggy Pop and Goran Bregovic,
> 'This Is a Film'

This book is an attempt to build a psycho-mantic map of social futurability: an inquiry (or divination) on the social becoming of the psychosphere.

From such a point of view we might see the lines of evolution issuing out from the present chaotic social mind's vibration.

This chaotic vibration is quite visible at the present, in the full-fledged epidemics of aggressive madness that surround us: Daesh, Donald Trump, financial austeritarianism and resurgent national-socialism are signs of contemporary psychotic epidemics.

Every day we experience the sense that opposition to the mounting wave of racism, fanaticism and the ensuing violence is pointless. In fact, this wave is not a political decision, the result of ideological and strategic elaboration, but the effect of despair, the reaction to long-lasting humiliation. The perfect rationality of the abstract computational machine, the inescapability of financial violence has jeopardized the consciousness and sensibility of the social organism, and frustration has reduced the general ability to feel compassion and to act empathically.

Madness? Although the genealogy of despair and aggression can be retraced to a social cause, I think that at the end of the day political reasoning is itself impotent. The only way to healing such emotional distress would be an emotional reactivation of the hidden potencies of the social organism: the Occupy! movement that deployed in 2011 has been the main attempt of our recent moment to summon all the energies of solidarity of which the social organism is capable. The outcome, however, of that movement was so poor that deception has destroyed any lingering sentiment of human solidarity, and the social organism is behaving like a beheaded body that still retains its physical energies but no longer possesses the ability to steer them in a reasonable direction.

I'm not sure that we can judge in psychopathological terms the dismantlement of modern social civilization. The economic interests of the corporations and the cynicism of politicians with no culture and no dignity have paved the way to the present explosion of madness.

Impotence is surely a symptom of disproportion: reason, that used to be the measure of the world (*ratio*), can no longer govern the hyper-complexity of the contemporary network of human relations.

This kind of disproportion may be labelled madness, in the sense of disorder, chaos, or mental mayhem. However, we must distinguish between different points of view when it comes to the definition of madness.

Is madness an exceptional occurrence that looms at the margins of the rational and reasonable daily business of life? Is it an inescapable disturbance of the ongoing conversation that holds society together?

If we reduce madness to a marginal, unavoidable disturbance that must be managed, that we have to placate and heal, we miss the point. Madness should not be seen as an accident to hide or to fix. Madness is the background of evolution, the chaotic matter that we are modelling and transforming into a provisional order.

Order means here a shared illusion of predictability, of regularity; a projective illusion that can hold for a short or a long period of time, a few minutes or perhaps centuries. An illusion that gives birth to what we call civilization.

We must distinguish two faces of madness: one is the factual meaninglessness of the world, the surrounding magma of matter, the uncontrollable proliferation of stimuli, the dazzling whirl of existence. This madness is the precondition of the creation of meaning: the groundless construction of knowledge, the invention of the world as a meaningful whole.

Then there is the subjective side of madness: the painful sentiment that things are flying away, the feeling of being overwhelmed by speed and noise and violence, of anxiety, panic, mental chaos.

Pain forces us to look for an order to the world that we cannot find, because it does not exist. Yet this craving for order does exist: it is the incentive to build a bridge across the abyss of entropy, a bridge between different singular minds. From this conjunction, the meaning of the world is evoked and enacted: shared semiosis, breathing in consonance.

The condition of the groundless construction of meaning is friendship. The only coherence of the world resides in sharing the act of projecting meaning: cooperation between agents of enunciation.

When friendship dissolves, when solidarity is banned and individuals stay alone and face the darkness of matter in isolation, then reality turns back into chaos and the coherence of the social environment is reduced to the enforcement of the obsessional act of identification.

There is something obsessional in this attempt to narrow the range of vibration out of which emerges possibility, and to reduce the unpredictability of future events.

> I could never know to what degree I was the perpetrator, configuring the configurations around me, oh, the criminal keeps returning to the scene of the crime! When one considers what a great number of sounds, forms reach us at every moment of our existence . . . the swarm, the roar, the river . . . nothing is easier than to configure! Configure! For a split second this word took me by surprise like a wild beast in a dark forest, but it soon sank into the hurly-burly of the seven people sitting here, talking, eating, supper going on.[9]

'De remi facemmo ala al folle volo', says Ulysses in Canto XXVI of *The Divine Comedy*.

> To the dawn
> Our poop we turn'd, and for the witless flight
> Made our oars wings, still gaining on the left.

The flight that leads to knowledge is foolish (witless), as it defies the established limits of reason.

The modern world comes out of the imprudence of the geographical explorations, from the desire to answer the question: where are the borders of the world?

The painful research of the picaresque swindler, who seeks to answer the unanswerable: who am I? Whence do I come?

The modern world results from the research of a non-theological order, and this research leads to the establishment of the bourgeois order whose measure (*ratio*) is time, labour and value accumulation.

This order was based on the semiotic organization and coding of the energies unchained by the explosion of the old Medieval theocratic order and by the enhancement of human experience that followed the technical innovations of printing books and traversing oceans. This order is the result of an act of nomination that gives meaning and scope to the evolving flows of information and discovery and technology.

Then entropy came and slowly dissolved that order: at the end of the capitalist cycle, the richness produced by labour is turned into misery and the freedom of knowledge is restricted by a new theology based on economic dogma. But the enforcement of dogma cannot replace the old bourgeois convention based on measure. When labour time and value start diverging, when the speed of info-stimulation is too fast for rational elaboration, then madness becomes the general language of the social system.

Capitalism is a dead dog, but society is unable to come out from under the rotting corpse, so the social mind is devoured by panic and furious impotence, until finally it turns to depression.

The social mind looks for a new form of semiotization

which might better adapt to the mutating composition of the world, but the vibration of its creation takes the form of a spasm, a frantic painful jolt of the soul and body itself.

Signs of the spasm can be detected all around, and the reaction to it assumes a variety of paranoid guises: Donald Trump boasts about the past glory of America and of reclaiming the legal use of torture. The European Union is torn apart by financial absolutism and nationalist aggression, and is building concentration camps for migrants on the coasts of Turkey, Egypt and Libya. An army of Muslim zealots behead innocent people, for God's sake. In the Philippines, a self-proclaimed murderer is elected president and calls for mass violence against social drop-outs.

Seventy years after Hitler's defeat, Hitler is back, multiplied by a dozen imitators, some of them are endowed with nukes.

The contours of the social convention have been swept away and unfiltered flows of imagination invade the social mind. The schizo runs in many directions as she sees the horizon of possibility, but she is unable to give shape to her pursuit of this horizon, so it forever eludes her.

In the last decades, the social mind has been taken in by a vortex of bipolar disorders: a long succession of euphoria and sadness have led to the present secular stagnation and to a state of steady depression.

The horizon of possibility is perceived as an infinite sprawl of connecting, flashing points. This perception generates anxiety and panic: the paranoid obsession with order tries to reduce the horizon to repetition, belonging and identity.

Power is based on the hypostatization of the existing relations of potency, on the surreptitious absolutization of the necessity implied in the existing *rapport de force*. Force crystallizes in a paranoid fixation to re-compact the world through rituals of identification. The relative necessity of the rule is arbitrarily transformed into absolute necessity: absolute capitalism is based on this deceptive trick of logic. Accumulation, profit and growth are surreptitiously turned into natural laws, and the field of economics legitimises this deception.

When society enters a phase of crisis or approaches collapse, we can glimpse the horizon of possibility. This horizon itself is hard to distinguish, and the territory that borders this horizon is hard to describe or to map.

The horizon of possibility can be best described by the words of Ignacio Matte Blanco in defining the unconscious: 'The unconscious deals with infinite sets that have not only the power of the enumerable but also that of the continuum.'[10]

The explosion of the semiotic sphere, the utter intensification of semiotic stimulation, has provoked simultaneously an enhancement of the horizon of possibility and a panic effect in the social neuro-system.

In this condition of panic, reason becomes unable to master the flow of events or to process the semio-stimulations released into the Infosphere. A schizophrenic mode spreads across the social mind, but this distress is double edged: it is painfully chaotic, but can also be seen as the vibration that precedes the emergence of a new cognitive rhythm.

According to D.E. Cameron, schizophrenia may be defined as an over-inclusive mode of interpretation.[11] Schizophrenic thought, in fact, appears to 'over include' various irrelevant objects and environmental cues in the interpretation of an enunciation: the schizo seems to be unable to limit attention to task-relevant stimuli because of an excessive broadening of the meaning of signs and of events.

This is why Guattari sees the schizo as the bearer of paradigmatic change (of 'chaosmosis', in Guattari's parlance). The schizo in fact is the person who has lost the ability to perceive the limits of metaphoric enunciation and tends therefore to take the metaphor as a description. The schizo, then, is the agent of a trans-rational experiment which may lead to the surfacing of an entirely new rhythm.

We may call this dimension 'chaotic' because it does not correspond to the existing laws of order, nevertheless the possible emerges from this sphere of chaos.

The intuition of an infinity of possibility is the source of contemporary panic, what can be described as a painful spasm. In Guattari, however, the spasm has a chaosmic side: from chaotic hyper-intensity, a new cosmos is poised to emerge.

I
POTENCY

In the first part of this book, I retrace the modern genealogy of the concept of potency, starting from the present condition of prevailing impotence of the action of men. I start from deciphering the meaning of Obama's trajectory. With all his extraordinary intellectual and political capabilities (certainly superior to those of the average specimen of the US political class), he has attempted to demonstrate that reason and political skill have the potency to implement hope, and to heal the wounds of American society and of the world. The final lesson of this experience, however, is impotence. Impotence is the keyword of this book, because impotence is the shape that potency takes in the age of technical and geopolitical hyper-complexity.

The re-emerging cult of nation and ethnicity, as exposed by the ascent of Donald Trump and the proliferation of macho-fascist dictators worldwide, is the backlash of the perception of impotence. Violence is replacing political mediation because political reason is determined to be devoid of potency.

The white middle class is unable to understand and control the hyper-complexity of financial automatisms, and this fuels sentiments of social impotence.

At same time, the military systems of the West are unable to defeat or contain terrorism. The sense of impotence is expressed by a frightening rise in white supremacism, melded with frustrated supre-machism: 'Make America Great Again'.

In this first part of the book, I retrace the philosophical genealogy of the present depression of the Western mind: after reading Schopenhauer and Heidegger from the point of view of white male decline, I try to situate the narrative imagination of Houellebecq in the same framework.

And finally, I try to elaborate on the senescence of the Western population, in which the energy-centred style of modernity is replaced by impotence and a sense of inadequacy.

1

The Age of Impotence

And indeed there will be time
For the yellow smoke that slides along the street,
Rubbing its back upon the window-panes;
There will be time, there will be time
To prepare a face to meet the faces that you meet;
There will be time to murder and create,
And time for all the works and days of hands
That lift and drop a question on your plate;
Time for you and time for me,
And time yet for a hundred indecisions,
And for a hundred visions and revisions,
Before the taking of a toast and tea.
In the room the women come and go
Talking of Michelangelo.

T.S. Eliot, 'The Love Song of J. Alfred Prufrock'

The Exorcism That Failed

I had trusted Obama. At the end of the summer of 2008, when the order of the world was shaking – the Bush wars were turning to catastrophe, and the big banks were collapsing – I thought that the new American president was heralding the emergence of a new possibility, a new future. I'm not so naïve as to believe in fairy tales, and I knew the cultural background of Barack Obama as that of a reasonable neoliberal who belongs to the privileged elite. But as I compared him with the ignorant, cynical clan of warmongers who had been in power before him, I thought that his ideas and his agenda were poised to open the way for a new age of peace and social justice.

The world had come to be acquainted with the young Obama in 2004, when he dared to say no to the Iraq War. His face, his nonchalant look, his alien beauty, his elegant multiracial lineaments made me think of a post-political leader, of an American intellectual announcing the post-national era, in which ethnic identities melt and give birth to a culturally global humanity.

Yes, a black president was a sign from above for someone who grew up in the '60s like me. In the past century we, the good communists (yes, there are good communists; I met a lot of them), had tried to emancipate the world from violence, war, exploitation. Certainly, we did not succeed. The bad communists were unmistakably more influential than us.

We had not succeeded, this is true. The socialist way has been trashed by totalitarian Bolsheviks and by subservient social-democrats.

Now was it the turn for someone like Obama? Maybe so, I told myself.

The force of events seemed to be ripe; the first black president was in the right situation to be led to do what people like me have failed to do in the twentieth century.

War has proven to be a horrible thing that generates more horrors, a defeat for everybody. And Obama was fully accredited to say so, after saying no to the invasion of Iraq conceived by the Bush regime, unlike his opponent in the 2008 Democratic primaries, Hillary Rodham Clinton, who did not dare to reject the patriotic call. He seemed, therefore, in the position to prevent future wars.

The collapse of Lehman Brothers and the crisis of subprime mortgages, in my expectation, set the conditions for changing the regime of financial capitalism.

He came to the fore with the slogan 'Yes We Can', and this was not irrelevant. Why should a politician say that, 'Yes We Can'? Is not America already the most powerful country in the world? Is not the president of the United States already the most powerful man on Earth? Is not politics the dimension in which power is exerted?

So why would he need to remind us that 'Yes We Can'?

Those three words were not an obvious declaration at all. That was a very strong statement, evidence that the man was smart and had zeroed in on the true problem. Obama knew that Americans wanted to be reassured on this point: we can. We have power therefore we can. Despite everything, we can: we can come out of the spiral of war, we can close Guantanamo, we can cancel the barbaric legacy of the Bush years, we can thwart the invading power of finance, we can end the history of racism and violence of the American police.

Nowadays, as I write these lines, eight years have passed from the pledge that was as much an exorcism as a promise.

The exorcism has failed, the promise has not been kept.

'By any objective measurement, his presidency has been perhaps the most consequential since Franklin Roosevelt's time,' wrote Timothy Egan.[1]

'To be fair', wrote Paul Krugman,

> Some widely predicted consequences of Obama's re-election didn't happen. Gasoline prices didn't soar. Stocks didn't plunge. The economy didn't collapse, in fact the US economy has now added more than twice as many private-sector jobs under Obama that it did over the same period of George Bush administration, and the unemployment rate is a full point lower that the rate Mitt Romney promised to achieve by the end of 2016.[2]

Undeniably Obama has been the most consequential president of the United States for a long time. Nevertheless, war is scaling again, more dangerous and demented than ever. Guantanamo is still there, more shameful than ever. Weapons are still on sale in every American town, despite the rampages at Columbine, Newton, Aurora, and who knows how many more. Rates of polluting emissions are growing while climate change is far from receding and Americans do not seem prone to reduce energy consumption. And the American people are more intolerant than ever, more quick to hate. The American unconscious is raucously reacting to the scandal of a black president, and an obtuse, violent form of racism is spreading, while the number of black people killed by police has clearly shown that black lives do not matter so much. White middle-aged workers are swamped by unemployment and hyper-exploitation, by depression and by loneliness. Heroin is raging in rural areas and overdoses are killing more than ever.

After the rescue of the banking system, notwithstanding the rise in taxes on high incomes and the remarkable results in the creation of jobs, workers are still paid less and less in America, as they are everywhere in the Western world.

Every second day someone speaks of recovery and of job creation. The truth is unemployment is on the rise all over the world except in America, but in America labour is more and more precarious, less and less rewarded.

During the Obama presidency a new social movement emerged in America which peacefully occupied public spaces such as Zuccotti Park, in close proximity to the New York Stock Exchange, where they named themselves Occupy Wall Street. And there was no happy ending. Just one year after the occupation of Zuccotti Park, Hurricane Sandy whipped through Manhattan and devastated its poor residents and those of its neighbouring boroughs. Some Occupy Wall Street activists created Occupy Sandy, an effort to provide organized relief efforts, implying by their action that we have been left only catastrophes to occupy.

Today if you go to Zuccotti Park, beware of police: gatherings of more than three people are forbidden.

Everywhere social life is pillaged by those who hold the financial levers, wherever society is unable to defend itself against those who would pillage.

And identitarian aggression is spreading everywhere. White racism is clearly resurfacing in the US, where KKK-like aggressions against black people have become a daily litany.

I had trusted Obama, but now, as his second term expires, I'm sad to say that his performance has persuaded me that political hope is over. At a certain point, Obama changed his philosophy from the hopeful 'Yes We Can' of 2008 to a cynical 'Don't Do Anything Stupid'.

Okay, I told myself, 'Don't Do Anything Stupid' is a pragmatic compromise considering the complexity of the contemporary world. Then, I witnessed the final sinking of his presidency when the Supreme Court rejected a plan to shield millions of undocumented immigrants from deportation and give them the right to work legally in the United States. And then, his administration's unconscionable cooperation with the president of Mexico in the act of deporting Central American refugees.

Obama and Peña Nieto have cooperated for two years to intercept desperate Central American refugees in southern Mexico, long before they can reach the U.S. border. These refugees are then typically deported to their home countries – which can be a death sentence.

The American–Mexican collusion began in 2014 after a surge of Central Americans crossed into the U.S., including 50,000 unaccompanied children. Obama spoke with Peña Nieto 'to develop concrete proposals' to address the flow. This turned out to be a plan to intercept Central Americans near Mexico's southern border and send them home. Washington committed $86 million to support the program. Although Obama portrayed his action as an effort to address a humanitarian crisis, he made the crisis worse. The old routes minors took across Mexico were perilous, but the new ones adopted to avoid checkpoints are even more dangerous.

The victims of this policy, deported in some cases to their deaths, are refugees like Carlos, a 13-year-old with a scar on his forehead from the time a gang member threw him to the ground in the course of executing his uncle.

In the last five years, Mexico and the U.S. have deported 800,000 people to Central America, including 40,000 children, according to the Migration Policy Institute. Last year, Mexico deported more than five times as many unaccompanied children as it had five years earlier, and the Obama administration heralds this as a success.[3]

Is my hero a coward? Is Obama a cynical and cruel careerist who gave away his principles and his moral values in exchange for his position? I don't think so. Fundamentally, I think humiliation has made him desperate.

Fundamentally, I think that we have to meditate on his experience and acknowledge that democracy is over, that political hope is dead. Forever.

Writing and Surfing

I should not write as if I was surfing the wave of this age: it is too dangerous, and I know it. Nevertheless, I cannot renounce the pleasure (the ambiguous and self-defeating pleasure) of interpreting signs that are not yet detectable, and processes that are still deploying.

So, this book is an attempt to map the currents of tidal change.

We are shifting from the Age of Thatcher to the Age of Trump – this is my general interpretation of the present becoming of the world. An anti-global front of so-called populist regimes is taking shape in the Western world, in the space of the demographical and economic decline of the white race (when I employ this word, I know that it has no scientific foundation but I also know that it can act as a powerful political mythology). The election of Trump to the presidency of the United States is the point of no return in the worldwide conflict between capitalist globalism and reactionary anti-globalism.

After the Treaty of Versailles, German society was suddenly impoverished and subjected to a long-lasting humiliation. In that situation, Hitler found his opportunity and his winning move consisted in urging Germans to identify as a superior race, not a humiliated class of exploited workers. This claim worked then and is working again now on a much larger scale: Donald Trump and Vladimir Putin, Jarosław Kaczyński and Viktor Orbán, Marine Le Pen and Boris Johnson, and many more small politicians of mediocre culture who smell the opportunity to win power by embodying the white race's will to potency in the wake of its decline.

The racial call is getting stronger, so much so that Boris Johnson calls Obama 'part-Kenyan', and racial fear motivates the anti-migrant policy of the European Union. The emergent racism is a legacy of colonialism combined with the social defeat of the working class in the Western world.

Frightening as it may be, the trend that I detect in the present becoming of the world is the unification of a heterogeneous front of anti-global forces, the resurgence of national-socialism and a widespread reaction against the decline of the white race perceived as the effect of globalization. As the social reference of the reactionary fronts that are winning all over the world is the defeated white working class, I would rather speak of national-workerism.

Mario Tronti has labelled industrial workers a 'rude pagan class' that fights for material interests and not for rhetorical ideals. It is for the sake of material interests the rude class of industrial workers is now turning nationalist and racist, as it did in 1933. Trump has won because he represents a weapon in the hands of impoverished workers, and because the left has delivered them into the hands of financial capital otherwise weaponless. Unfortunately, this weapon will soon be turned against the workers themselves, and lead them towards racial warfare.

This Euro-American anti-global racist front is certainly the fruit of thirty years of neoliberal governance. But until yesterday, in Europe as in the United States the conservatives were globalist and neoliberal. No more.

The looming war is already being defined as fighting along three different fronts. The first front is the neoliberal power that is tightening its grip on governance, pursuing the agenda of austerity and privatization. The second front is the anti-global Trumpism based on white resentment and working-class despair. The third front, taking place largely backstage, is the growing necro-empire of terrorism, in all its different shapes of religious bigotry, national rage and economic strategy, that I identify as necro-capital.

I think that the War on Terror, whose main target is the global jihad, will sooner or later give way to the war between capitalist globalism and worldwide anti-global nationalsocialism (that may be named 'Putin-Trumpism').

Democracy Will Not Come Back

I do not identify impotence as powerlessness. Often when lacking power, people have been able to act autonomously, to create forms of self-organization and to subvert the established power. In this age of precariousness, powerless people have been unable to create effective forms of social autonomy, unable to implement voluntary change, unable to pursue change in a democratic way, because democracy is over.

One of the final nails in the coffin of democracy came in the summer of 2015, when the democratically elected, anti-austerity government of Greece was obliged to bend to financial blackmail. In the very place where democracy had been invented twenty-five centuries ago, democracy was suspended. Rather, what we in the European Union are facing is not merely provisional suspension of democracy, but the final replacement of politics with a system of techno-financial automatism.

Expecting the revivification of democracy and fighting for such a goal would be futile because the very conditions for the effectiveness of political reason (and particularly of democratic politics) have since dissolved. I'm not talking here of a political or a military defeat, or a battle that was lost. Many times in the course of modern history the good guys have been defeated; they have resisted, have recovered and, in the end, have achieved what they needed by playing and winning the democratic game. But I think that this will not happen again.

The systemic conditions for democracy have been cancelled by prevailing irreversible processes. Irreversible is the enslavement of immaterial labour because the global labour market requires boundless competition among workers and pre-emption of any social solidarity. Irreversible is the moral and psychological misery of a generation of children who have learned more words from an electronic screen than from a human voice. Irreversible is the melting of the Arctic ice, and irreversible is the spiral of economic competition and military aggression.

The conditions for democracy are two (at least): freedom and effectiveness of political volition. Both have been dismantled. Since language has been subjected to the rule of the technic, and techno-linguistic automatism has taken hold of social relations, freedom has become an empty word, and political action has grown ineffective and inconsequential. Hoping for the revivification of the values, principles and expectations of democracy is therefore a self-deception, because true decision has been absorbed by the connective machine, and popular rage has been organized instead by nationalist and racist parties.

The psycho-cognitive constitution of the neo-humans (their cognitive hardware, I mean) cannot support the software of the past humanist culture, so words like 'freedom', 'equality', 'fraternity' have lost their situational meaning.

Can the beginning of this mutation be precisely dated? Obviously not. However, I will arbitrarily assign to it the year 1977.

That same year many interesting things happened. In Silicon Valley, Steve Wozniak and Steve Jobs created the Apple trademark. In London, Sid Vicious cried 'No Future'. In Italian cities, the last proletarian rebellion of the last century and the first precarious rebellion of the new century went on stage.

Since then we have witnessed something deeper than a change, a transformation or a revolution: we have witnessed a mutation of the molecular composition of the human and of the social organism. Technology has altered the composition of the chemical matter composing the atmosphere, of the semiotic substances composing the Infosphere, and finally of the psycho-cognitive modes of elaboration. This is why political reversibility is impossible, why voluntary action has turned impotent: volition has no bearing when facing irreversible processes.

Conscious volition cannot dismantle the heavy machines that have provoked these irreversible changes: mutation has perfused and rearranged the human mind, and has consequently disempowered consciousness, volition and action.

A sort of palsy has in this way taken possession of the conscious organism. Cognitive and emotional dissonance results from the inability of conscious behaviour to oppose evil. So, we sense our own impotence and are led to think that our suffering cannot be relieved by political projects, but only by psychopharmacology.

Imagination

What about our imagination of the future in this age of impotence?

Let us go to the movies. Dystopia has taken centre stage in show business: Hollywood blockbusters bring us a perception of the future which is simultaneously violent and depressing.

The *Hunger Games* series is one of the most impressive financial successes ever in cinema history. Young people are the bulk of the audience for the series, as they were for the books on which they are based. The future world they depict is ethically repugnant and intolerable for the human consciousness, so much so that a naïve viewer might interpret the film as a sort of radical political denunciation of social precariousness and of the violence provoked by the militarization of economic power. Nothing, however, is more removed from the intentions of its creators, and, more importantly, from the way the young moviegoers receive and decode its message. The teenager who goes to see the *Hunger Games*, precarious, unemployed, impoverished by the crisis as she may be, does not draw from the movie the conclusion that we should rebel and stop the barbaric transformation it imagines. In the film, there is, finally, a rebellion that occurs, but it is something sad and hopeless, whose outcome contradicts any idea of possible solidarity among the oppressed.

The young viewer does not draw the lesson that he should rebel against the current state of affairs, but rather is persuaded that the *Hunger Games* describes the world he will inhabit, in which everybody will be obliged to live in the near future. In this new world, only the winner can survive, and if one wants to win she must eliminate all the others, friends and foes.

Acts of solidarity may occur in the *Hunger Games*. For instance, the protagonist, Katniss Everdeen, enters the violent contest in order to save her sister from a near-certain death. But this is the solidarity of despair, the solidarity of people who cannot even imagine a life of peace, let alone one of happiness.

The majority of video games teach the same lesson. Beyond their narrative content, sensorial stimulation is training young people to compete, to fight, to win or to disappear. The morals on which these video game are based is the idea that the machine is always winning, and only those who interrupt its rhythm can defeat competitors.

In real life, everybody is a competitor, and the lover on Sunday night may be a competitor on Monday morning.

The *Hunger Games*, not dissimilarly, mobilizes the ludic attention of the connective generation, but not for a persuasive or ideological function. Rather, they have a function of psycho-cognitive moulding: a plastic effect, not through moral content, but through nervous stimulation.

The psychology and the cognitive reactivity of the precarious generation is led to internalize the perception of social life as a field of war, a place where everybody is a winner or a loser, is eliminator or is eliminated, a space where solidarity and empathy are only dangerous distractions weakening the warrior that you are obliged to be.

Thought is a self-defeating act because thinking slows one's reactions, and slowness makes you prey in the game in which every other player is also trying to eliminate you.

A Tragedy for the Human Civilization

According to Mario Tronti, one of the most important thinkers of Italian *operaismo*, 'the workers' defeat has been a tragedy for the human civilization.'[4]

In the short term, the fall of the communist project has provoked a global collapse of late modern welfare, but from the point of view of long-term evolution, it has opened the door to a wave of barbarianism that endangers modern humanism itself.

The short-term consequences are easy to identify: the working class has not disappeared after the defeat; far from it, the industrial army has expanded worldwide, as huge concentrations of industrial production have emerged in newly industrialized countries. But the working class has been dispossessed of any political force, and stripped of any tools for self-defence as it is now composed of temporary aggregations of precarious labourers who are not allowed to create a community of solidarity within a process of continuous deterritorialization.

In a very short space of time, industrial concentration can be displaced from one region of the world to another, and no union or political organization can effectively oppose this act of aggressive delocalization. Long-existing structures of solidarity can be dismantled overnight because of the deregulation that has dismantled any legal protection of the community, of the territory and of the workers.

Wage conditions are now unilaterally determined by capitalists: as a consequence, salaries have been halved in the last decades and the industrial system is regressing to proto-industrial conditions. More generally, the living conditions of society are rapidly deteriorating. Access to education, health care and leisure time were social rights won by unionized struggles: as a consequence of their political defeat, society is going back to a condition of misery and dependency, while mass ignorance is resurfacing.

It's difficult to ignore this regression, but neoliberal applauders have an easy reply for those who, like me, lament the Western depression: they say that Chinese, Indonesian, and African workers now have the possibility of buying a car or a cell-phone. This is true.

They use their car to go to the factory; they use their cell-phone to call their families when they are forced to migrate in search of a job. Those who get the opportunity to be exploited in an industrial factory have access to the sphere of consumption. However, if we look closer at the social evolution of the new proletarians, it's easy to understand that when they were poor they were not so poor as they are now: deprived of their communities, divested of solidarity, stripped of leisure time and obliged to sustain fatigue, stress and competition.

On a global scale, the social condition has worsened enormously since the disappearnace of socialist hope, but the rise in exploitation and existential misery is not the only consequence of the defeat of the workers' movement. The other consequence is war. War is expanding its hold on the lives of people: they are more and more wars of the poor against the poor, religious and ethnic wars fuelled by despair. The plague of nationalism is back, more and more dominating the life of populations, as an effect of the workers' defeat and of the extinction of internationalism.

In the first years of the new century, a movement for peace spread worldwide: on 15 February 2003, millions of people marched against American aggression in Iraq. The day after this demonstration, the largest of all time, President Bush sarcastically announced, 'I'm not going to decide policy based upon a focus group. The role of a leader is to decide policy based upon, in this case, the security of the people.'

We know what happened next. Bush had his war, he declared that it was an endless war, and now, more than ten years later, there is still no end in sight. That day exposed the fundamental weakness of the peace movement.

I marched with the peace movement on 15 February 2003, and I'll march with pacifists any time they call. But I also know marching is useless: pacifism is the symptom and the measure of our impotence. In fact, only internationalism is the condition by which we can effectively pursue peace. Internationalism is not a disposition of the mind, not a will for peace or a refusal of war. It is something much deeper and much more concrete. It's the consciousness that people worldwide have the same interests and the same motivation. Internationalism (as rhetorical as this may seem) is the solidarity of workers regardless of their nation, race or religion.

But the moment of internationalist consciousness is over. German workers are pitted against Greek workers, Turkish workers against Kurdish workers, and Sunni workers against Shiite workers. They have been obliged to forget about their shared reality as workers.

The workers' defeat is a huge, historic tragedy, Tronti writes. According to him they 'have lost because they have been unable to become the State.'

I think the contrary is true.

Communism turned into a totalitarian nightmare because Leninism pushed workers to take hold of the state, to identify with the socialist state, so the statalization of the working class has paralysed the social dynamics and has forced the autonomous process of social emancipation into a fixed political structure.

In the Soviet empire, the result has been a miserable society and an authoritarian state: real communism has cancelled the possible communism that was inscribed in the social composition of work, and in the autonomy of the general intellect.

The Frigid Game

As connective engines are embedded in the general intellect, the social body is separated from its brain.

Subjected to the rules of work – precarious and fractured – cognitive activity becomes part of a process of cooperation that is disembodied and deterritorialized.

This is why the social body has lost contact with its brain: the production of knowledge and technology is deployed in a privatized corporate space which is disconnected from the needs of society, and responds only to economic requirements of profit maximization.

Disconnected from the body, the social brain becomes incapable of autonomy.

Disconnected from the brain, the social body becomes incapable of strategy or empathy.

Within the new dimension of networked production, the individual body is simultaneously exposed to constant intensification of neural stimulation, and insulated from the physical presence of others: everyone lives in the same condition of nervous electrostimulation. The hyper-stimulated body is simultaneously alone and hyper-connected: the more it is connected, the more it is alone.

The social corporeality, however, cannot be dissolved, so it resurfaces, de-cerebrated and disconnected from intellectual cooperation, unable to pursue a common strategy.

The technical subsumption of cognitive activity is based on the ability to capture attention.

At the end of the '70s the first video games appeared on the market.

In the bars of Italian cities, electronic video games replaced the old mechanical pinball machines. Video games came in large metal boxes, with coloured screens where small green aliens invaded Earth and warriors in black responded with weapons flashing. Sooner or later the game ended and two fatal words appeared on the screen: game over.

In that kind of primordial video game, the machine always eventually won, regardless of the ability or speed of the player.

Machines playing against their human creators, and winning, as their human creator had built the game in such a way that the machine could not be defeated. Now we live in the world of embedded game over: the automaton is winning by design.

But who is the designer?

The designer is the recombinant force of millions of cognitarians who cooperate within the game, but remain alone outside the game.

They are cooperatively running the process of innovation, invention and implementation of knowledge, but they do not know each other. The cooperating brains have no collective body and the private bodies have no collective brain.

I remember those days when, in a bar in Naples, I played *Last Safety for Alpha*: the announcement of the future carried by the first generation of video games was fascinating and frightening as well.

Then came the time of impotence. The overall rhythm of information has accelerated. Those flows are perceived as neural stimuli by the conscious organism, while the sensory organism lives in a permanent state of nervous electrostimulation and bodily contraction.

As consciousness and emotion need time for personal elaboration, and as time is short, attention becomes disconnected from consciousness and from emotion. Herein originates the contemporary emotional distress.

Dyschronia: a malady of duration, a pathology of 'lived time'.[5]

The epidemic of attention deficit disorder is a symptom of this dyschronia: children who grow up in the info-saturated space show signs of nervous hyper-motility. Only for instants can they focus on an object of attention. Their focus tends to shift too fast for learning, for expression, or for affection.

In a condition of hyper-stimulation, the cognitive organism cannot process the emotional content of the stimuli.

Sexual impotence has a similar aetiology.

Stimulation frequency and diffusion, the speed of exposure of the self to the erotic stimulus have accelerated to a point that it is more and more difficult to decode consciously emotional messages or to process them with the needed tenderness. Our time has grown short, narrow, contracted, so the stimulus hardly translates into desire, and desire hardly translates into conscious contact, and contact hardly translates into pleasure.

The sex-appeal of inorganic matter that electronics has inserted between bodies has resulted in a sort of widespread sexualization of the environment and in the physical isolation of the bodies.

The insertion of the inorganic (electronic) in communication among bodies acts as a disturbance. This is why pleasure seems to be replaced by adrenal discharge. The massive consumption of pharmacological products that prolong the male erection in absence of desire does not only happen among the elderly. There are reasons to think that, more than merely a physical problem, people who take erectile dysfunction pills do so for the psychological problem of time scarcity and emotional distress.

Sexual inattention is a side effect of the wide process of the technical subjection of our attention span. The porno explosion, the massive consumption of pornographic images, is part of this cycle. We are exposed to a flow of erotic images, mixed in and among a flow of advertising, entertainment and so on. These flows are ceaselessly mobilizing our emotional and erotic reactivity. Our attention is under permanent demand, but is unable to focus on a particular object.

A sort of frigidity is simultaneously induced in the sensuous sphere by the permanent electrostimulation of the organism, by the insertion of electronic devices in the continuum of the bodily sphere. By frigid, I do not refer to anorgasmic behaviour or similar dysfunction of sexual pleasure: I refer to a widespread condition of anaesthesia following continuous tension, and a leaning towards depression.

In the book *Impuissances*, Yves Citton takes into account a wide range of French literary works that deal with sexual impotence. In the chapter 'Le Fiasco', Citton identifies the 'cause' of the *défaillance* (incapacity) as the excess of stimulation that the male subject is unable to master. 'It is not a lack of attraction, but rather the excess of beauty by which the woman is perceived as untouchable.'[6]

Rhythm acceleration, stimulus intensification, hyperstimulation of the nervous system: this is a likely pathway to sexual failure. And in the context of patriarchal culture, which is the deep background of Western civilization – sex and social power are narrowly intertwined.

> Grounding his identity on the arousing as a proof of existence, the male is condemned to reduce his self-assurance on something quite episodic . . . The self-reputation of the person who grounds identity on virility is obliged to assume a posture of Omnipotence.[7]

In many regards, impotence may be viewed as a problem of rhythm: the relation between embodied time and automated time intensifies. Because of hyper-stimulation, the investment in desire is increased, up to the point of exhaustion. Then the sensuous organism withdraws the investment in desire, and surfs the icy waves of the lake of frigidity.

The aestheticization of contemporary culture may be read as a symptom and a metaphor of frigidity: endless flight from one object of desire to another, overload of aesthetic stimulation, invasion of the public space by aesthetically arousing advertising.

In *Carnage*, the claustrophobic Roman Polanski movie, Kate Winslet's character, Nancy Cowan, explains that her husband, a lawyer continuously answering calls on his smart phone, thinks every stimulation coming from a distant agent is more exciting and important than any stimulation coming from the living beings who dwell in his vicinity.

The present shifts away, impossible to touch or to savour, as the flows of neuro-stimulation push forward, towards a never-coming future. The emotion that comes from the near body is blurred by frantic impulses coming from afar, continuously reclaiming our attention.

Anaesthesia is the effect of sensory saturation and the path to an-empathy: the ethical catastrophe of our time is based on the inability to perceive the other as a sensible extension of one's own sensibility.

The cognitive competence that we call sensibility has developed as the ability to decipher signs that do not belong to the verbal sphere. This competence is under threat as cognitive automatisms inscribed in the digital exchange (and reinforced by the economic code) tend to reduce the conscious elaboration to a succession of binary choices.

In psychopathological parlance, autistic persons do not have a 'theory of the other's mind'.[8] When acting inside a network of automatic exchanges, it is not necessary to assume the existence of the other's mind or to interpret signs as if they were from another conscious and sensitive organism. Within this context, signs need only be interpreted according to a finite computation of a discrete set of information. The other is only a simulated construction of the interaction between our mind and the machine. Compatibility replaces sensibility.

The connective biosphere is the smooth space where information, the now-universal substance of valorization, can easily flow. But in order to flow without obstruction, it is necessary to remove any impurity that may slow its path: namely, sensibility.

The connective paradigm (and the connective mode) infiltrates the deep fabric of the human biosphere, permeates the organism's barriers, and something happens at the level of the process of individuation. The mutation invades the individual's self-perception, and integrates it in the connective framework of the socio-technical continuum of the net.

The individual organism is cleared of any mark of

singularity and transformed into a smooth surface, free of roughness, of irregularity, and therefore compliant with the linguistic machine, with the hub of techno-linguistic automatisms.

Connective individuation fractures cells of a process of modular recombination. The bio-informatic superorganism reads the event of language as a disturbance, and discards it as noise.

2

Humanism, Misogyny and Late Modern Thought

Humanism as Potency and Freedom

An exhaustive definition of humanism is beyond my scope here, but by the word 'humanism' we generally refer to a philosophical and artistic movement that appeared first in Italy in the fifteenth century, then spread throughout Europe. However, in this context, I refer particularly to a concept that widely defines the identity of European culture in modern times.

Here, I propose to consider humanism as the assertion of freedom and the potency of man.

According to Leon Battista Alberti, man has been created for work (*opera*), and usefulness is humanity's determination. The humanist emphasis on activity and enterprise (*intrapresa*) implies two conceptual dimensions: freedom and potency of action.

The notion of freedom is not, here, intended in the juridical sense: it is not freedom from the law or from political constriction. It is instead ontological freedom, independence from predetermined forms, and, therefore, the possibility to create forms that do not pre-exist in the mind of God.

Humanism emancipates human history from the presence of a God no longer needed to explain human action. The form of things does not depend on the will of God, but on the action of man. Ernst Bloch, in his book on the philosophy of the Renaissance, speaks of the birth of the 'technical utopia'.

The humanist philosopher Francis Bacon resurrects the myth of Prometheus, the mythological Titan who gives men boundless potency and the ability to think of the future. Technology, the application of knowledge, can establish its power only when God starts to disappear. In the history of modern civilization, technology has now actually supplanted God, establishing a sort of technical theocracy.

Humanism started with an affirmation of the ontological independence of human action, but technology has acquired an all-pervading potency, up to the point of its ability to grow independent from its human creators, and of deploying itself as a system of automatisms.

According to Bloch, the world of the Renaissance reaffirmed the Greek cult of the man as a standing person, forgetting the kneeling Gothic forms of the theocratic past. But at the end of the modern age, the Gothic style has come back, and in late modern times, men are obliged to genuflect again in the hyper-Gothic buildings of the metropolis.

The perspective of the Renaissance projected a human order on the world, then the Baroque multiplied the points of view and the perspectives to the degree in which the complexity of the world surpassed the capacities of the rational government of the mind on the surrounding world. The Renaissance inaugurated the idea of the kingdom of man who gives order to the surrounding space according to the linear anthropocentric perspective. Then, the sudden enhancement of knowledge and the proliferation of points of view and of perspectives gives way to the Baroque sensibility well represented by the Leibniz phantasmagoria of the fold.

The Baroque spirit is haunted by the pervasive force of technique, and when the technique comes to occupy all the space of freedom, humanism loses its ground. Since the Romantic age, a nostalgia for authenticity takes central place in the philosophical sentiment: authenticity is identified as a feature of the pre-technical world. While enhancing the sphere of political freedom, modernity has eroded the ontological freedom of the past imagined authenticity. In this dynamic, I find the core of a thread of reactionary hyper-humanism that goes from Schopenhauer through Nietzsche and takes full shape in Heidegger.

The ambiguous legacy of Heidegger is deeply inscribed in the philosophical underpinnings of our time. A sort of reactionary refusal of modernization as a technical becoming of the world runs through the past century as a depressive line.

Heidegger envisioned the relation between technique and language as one of perverting influence; under his direction a nostalgic form of humanism has taken a front seat in the philosophical landscape.

Heidegger stands in the philosophical theatre of late modernity as a black magician, a bad alchemist who distils poisonous conceptual substances and injects them into the cultural perception. He was a small man with a limited horizon, an insensitive coward who transformed fear into conceptual pillars. The fear of technique led the man from Freiburg to think of the late modern condition (the age of the image of the world) as a lugubrious condition.

Humanity is reduced, in his view, to the authentic, and what he can see is only the twilight of authenticity, the dissolution of the small world in which he developed his own mundane experience.

The Heidegger vision of the world is lugubrious because lugubrious was his soul.

The work of Heidegger has gained great attraction in the critical thought of the late twentieth century because he conceptualized the dismay provoked by the decline of the humanistic world. But critical thought should emancipate itself from his technophobic charm if we want to be able to face the main challenge of our time. Far from rejecting the ambiguous legacy of technology, we have to re-program the relation between technology and life, starting in the sphere of work: the subjectivity of cognitive workers, their rebellion, their autonomy and their solidarity. Critical thought has to distinguish between the human and the authentic. The word 'authentic' means nothing: authenticity is based only on the limited memory of a generation, on the narrow perceptions of a territorial mind.

And we must also distinguish the human from humanism. Humanism is a vision of the human, but the human is not identical to that vision nor restricted to the humanist definition.

Language is larger than the rules that are inscribed in language by technical automation or by biology itself.

Movement

In this book about impotence, I want to talk about myself, my despair or, rather, my vision without hope. In recent years, I have published a book about the end of the future and another about suicide in the connective generation. Now I write a book about impotence. Some friends worry for me and suggest I take a vacation as they think I'm depressed.

The truth is different: my despair is based on an intellectual understanding of the failure of the promise of modernity that has nourished my formation, but I know, too, that announcing the failure of the intellectual enterprise that has motivated my life does not make me happy.

From an early age, I have mingled with social movements, taking part in many waves of social uprising because I think that, albeit defeated and despairing, movements are the carriers of a possibility that is not wholly extinguished.

This possibility is the liberation of knowledge and of technology from capital as Ultimate Gestalt. The subject of this possibility is the collective intelligence re-embodied in conditions of solidarity.

Simultaneously, I am aware that the conditions of solidarity do not exist at present. Connective intelligence is unfit to act as collective intelligence: it is unfit to activate solidarity, to share a bodily sphere of communication. Consequently, the conditions of social subjectivity do not yet give shape to the potency needed for the actualization of the possibility. But the possibility is there, hidden in the connection of countless brains that are presently obliged to cooperate only in order to increase the corporate profit, but are potentially suited for a different paradigm of social concatenation.

Inventing another model based on usefulness and not on valorization, building a social and technological platform aimed at the autonomy of the general intellect, aimed to deploy the use value of the general intellect – this is the agenda for the long period that can produce useful effects. This agenda is the movement.

What is the meaning of the word 'movement'? It is a question that I should answer, as I've been using that word so often over the last fifty years.

By the word 'movement' we mean, obviously, the displacement from one point to another in space. As an effect of the displacement, the viewer can see things she did not see before. We can see, therefore, that every movement produces an effect of knowledge, otherwise it is a false *bewegung*.

Sartre uses the expression a 'group in fusion' and Guattari speaks of a 'collective subject of enunciation'. 'Movement' is when a lot of people start to sing the same song without any musical score.

But the word 'movement' for me means something more: the full deployment of the potentialities contained in a collective body, the implementation of the technical and productive potency of a collective body – a potency that can deploy only when that body becomes a movement.

Philosophical Genesis of Reactionary Thought

I spent the year of 2011 in a condition of emotional, political and theoretical euphoria: the Occupy movement was spreading and promising to break the cage of financial abstraction. Then I witnessed its defeat. Actually, that defeat was simply the consequence of social impotence: the attempt to oppose the dismantlement of social welfare was doomed to failure because financial power was already entrenched in the social, psychological and linguistic structures of daily life.

After that defeat, I focused on studying the effects of the depression that followed the dissolution of the movement. The consciousness of living in a condition of abstract domination, the consciousness of the increasing control that technical automatisms are exerting on the social and cultural life of populations, has led me to develop a sense of aversion towards the potency of technology, and a sentiment of nostalgia for political freedom and for the authenticity of life. But I don't like these sentiments, I don't recognize them as a part of me. They have successfully conquered some part of my mind because I fear my own impotence. But this fear *is* the impotence: there is no impotence except in the fear of it.

My philosophical formation, my political experience and my personal character do conflict with these sentiments of reactionary nostalgia, and of fear of the process of post-human development.

These sentiments – that led me to write *Heroes*, a book devoted to the suicidal trend that is spreading in our times – are linked with the abysmal political defeat that the workers' movement and humanistic culture more generally have undergone in the last thirty years, but are also linked with the process of decline of my mind, of my body and my sexuality. I must consciously come to terms with impending senility, in order not to mistake this personal condition as universal.

I ask myself: how deeply have I been influenced by the reactionary philosophy that descends from the humanist critique of technique and from the nostalgia for authenticity? My intention is to disjoin the understanding of the crisis of humanism from the reactionary nostalgia conveyed by this understanding.

From a materialistic point of view, we see two different tendencies. The first tendency is implicit (as a possibility whose deployment is however unimaginable at present): it is a tendency towards full deployment of the general intellect, the possibility of an emancipation of technology from the semiotic context of capitalism, the liberation of time from salaried work, the revitalization of collective life, and the expansion of care, cultural education and research: a post-labourist renaissance.

The other tendency is towards the growing impoverishment of social life, the devastation of the mind and body of society, the psychological epidemic provoked by the hyper-exploitation of neural energies, and finally environmental and military suicide.

It's hard to escape the feeling that only the second tendency is prevailing. But the ambivalence of the present situation must be preserved, because in this ambivalence is hidden the way towards our emancipation. The task of free thought is to enable freedom, and freedom means autonomy from the blackmail of realism that forgets the inscribed possibility and only sees the forms of power currently deployed.

I want to retrace the lineage of that sort of reactionary thought that has submitted a critique to nostalgia, and absolutized the humanist model as the only expression of the human.

Perhaps depression is the best way to examine the truth of life and of history. However, the task of philosophy is not to certify the obvious truths.

The philosopher is compelled to tell the truth, without

reticence or denial. Then he must get free from the truth, and keep his mind open to the multiplicity of possibilities that power attempts to reduce to a single one.

The Body of the *Ich Denke*

Hegel conceived of history as the deployment of the totalizing design of the absolute Geist: in the modern age, individuals have identified themselves as historical actors because of the tension towards totality that was pervading their thought and their action. Without totalization, there is no history, in Hegel's view: the potency of action comes from the consistency of the actor's project and the self-fulfilling historical reason.

But the conscious action of the historical actors who have taken central stage in the modern drama has not fulfilled any rational order.

We are far from Hegel, back to the singularity of exist-ence, in a dimension that resembles the 'ego' of Max Stirner, without the pathos of unicity that one can find in Stirner's vision. If we want to retrace the genealogy of the existential-ist approach, and particularly of the concept of existential singularity (existential anarchism, as according to Federico Campagna in *The Last Night*), we have to refer to Arthur Schopenhauer.

So strongly do I dislike Schopenhauer that at a certain point of my life I decided that I did not want to read his books anymore. When I read somewhere that during the Berlin riots of 1848, this vile individual invited policemen to his house because from the windows of his living room it was possible to aim at workers demonstrating in the streets, I decided to expel his books from my library. Recently I had the chance to read *The Schopenhauer Cure* by Irvin D. Yalom. This novel is about a psychoanalyst who is going to die from cancer, but it also retraces the biography of Arthur Schopenhauer. Reading the book (quite entertaining indeed) I discovered many details that helped me to better understand this unpleasant fellow, and gave me a better grasp of the genesis of his thought.

It is often said, not without reason, that Schopenhauer anticipated crucial themes of psychoanalysis, but reading Yalom I discovered that we should psychoanalytically investigate the philosopher's biography if we want to comprehend the inner meaning of his work. His relationship with the mother is the key to his philosophical personality and his late modern sensibility. Johanna Schopenhauer was a cultivated, lively woman, who was married, without much enthusiasm, to Arthur's austere father, a rich merchant of little charm. When the old husband goes to glory, she is finally allowed to live the life that she has always desired: travelling, writing, meeting artists and intellectuals. But the son – clumsy, annoying, indelicate and sometimes rude – does not tolerate the joy and feminine freedom of his mother.

Arthur, at twenty years old, is aware that life is drawing Johanna away, and unable to come to terms with his abandonment, reacts with jealousy and male aggression. He goes after his mother, who has left Lübeck and is living in Frankfurt where she is friends with Wolfgang von Goethe. Arthur accuses her of squandering the family endowment, but, finally, Johanna writes him a letter: let me alone, please; get out of my sight. They never met again, but the identification with the father became in the young philosopher a sort of hatred for life, and in particular a declared hatred for women. The wealth accumulated by the father is being spent by the mother, and the order built by the man is dissolved by the body of the woman, who forgets self-sacrifice and subjection, and squanders the capital that should be preserved for the progeny. Actually, Johanna squanders nothing: she is a talented writer and does not undermine the family property. But in truth the dissipation that Arthur worries about is not financial.

After reading the novel, I decided to start re-reading Schopenhauer, which I'm doing now. This stingy and supercilious guy deserves, in the end, to be read because he is the first German thinker to deconstruct the Hegelian building exposing the falseness of idealism. He does so starting from the body: a stiffened body, a body contracted by avarice, fear of dissolution and misogyny.

The hatred of Schopenhauer towards Hegel is well known: Arthur went so far in his unfriendliness that when the University of Berlin offered him a chair, the presumptuous new professor decided to give lectures at the same time as the well-established professor Georg Wilhelm Frederich Hegel. The outcome was ludicrous: his lectures were deserted while Hegel's classroom was crowded.

Nevertheless, his critical stance was well founded: he was aiming at the core of Hegel's historical panlogism.

Schopenhauer categorically rejects as a consolation the vision of history as a tortuous path towards the perfect realization of reason. In order to dismantle this Hegelian vision, he refers to Kant, transforming Kantian philosophy into a sort of post-Hegelian materialism. As he wants to escape the idealistic circularity, Schopenhauer retraces the meaning of the Kantian *ich denke*. This is the point of problematization:

the meaning of *ich denke* is the transcendental constitution of the phenomenal world, and also the condition of possibility, of perception and of projection of the world as phenomenon and experience.

The world of phenomena does not pre-exist the act of thinking, but is established by it. Phenomena, in fact, are the objects of our experience that we can grasp only according to the transcendental forms of perceptive ability (*Transzendentale Apperzeption*). In Kant's parlance, 'transcendental' means preceding experience, and therefore devoid of empirical content.

In *The World as Will and Representation*, Schopenhauer reflects on the double face of the *ich denke*: the act of thinking makes perceivable the known world of experience, and no experience precedes the act of thinking.

Hegel had already criticized the Kantian *Vernunft* as empty universality with no subjectivity, and had transformed reason into a historical process of self-affirmation of the subject, which is the mediation of the absolute Geist.

Schopenhauer goes in a different direction that is more interesting to me.

After agreeing with Kant that the world we know is a phenomenon, he wants to understand where the subject of knowledge comes from. 'Everything that exists for knowledge, and hence the whole of this world, is only object in relation to the subject, perception of the perceiver, in a word, representation,' he writes.[1] The world is representation as it is the projection of a representing will; following Husserl, we may say that the world is the projection of an intentionality which is simultaneously transforming and representing.

But Schopenhauer does not stick to the Kantian lesson, and questions further the lack of determination of the transcendental subject. The *ich denke* lacks a body. We should give a body to Kant's act of thinking, so he will no more be a winged angelical head without body.

The individual body can be viewed under two different perspectives: on one hand, it is an object among other objects, a phenomenon, a representation projected in the world by the intentionality of the transcendental subject. But it is simultaneously the organic proliferating living and historical materiality that feeds the activity of knowledge.

> The meaning of the world that is in front of me as an effect of my representation, could never be grasped if the observer was only a pure knowledge subject, a winged angelical head without body. But this subject has roots in the world, and in it finds itself as a person. Knowledge, which is a condition of the world itself as representation, happens completely through the body – whose affections are the beginning of the intellectual intuition of that world.[2]

> This actual world of what is knowable, in which we are and which is in us, remains both the material and the limit of our consideration.[3]

Schopenhauer argues that knowledge presupposes a knowing subject and a known object: but the object of knowledge and the body are both objects that we know and the subjects of the process of knowledge. The *ding-an-sich* of corporeality is beyond the ability of our knowledge.

Denouncing the limits of the Kantian transcendental subject – the lack of bodily grounding – Schopenhauer undertakes the beginning step towards materialism. In his critique of Kant, he moves in a direction that is the opposite of Hegel's.

In order to overcome Kant, Hegel inscribes the subject in the spiritual historical becoming, as momentum on the pathway towards the triumph of the Absolute Spirit. Schopenhauer, instead, grounds the intentionality of representation in a body, in bodily affections. The Spinozian affection comes back as a pulsating body of thinking subjectivity.

But Schopenhauer looks like a sort of dark Spinoza: whereas Spinoza envisioned the body as an open, boundless field of possibilities, Schopenhauer circumscribes the body as impotence. For him our disgrace lies in our will: the will can never be satisfied. Therefore, we never stop willing, and life is a ceaseless suffering because it is only the phenomenon of will, the will objectified.

Schopenhauer determined that the body is at the origin of the thinking act (*ich denke*), but after this, the only thing he is able to say is that this corporeality is 'for death', and that love vanishes as soon as the object of love is revealed (an old male-chauvinist prejudice).

By what criterion do we express a judgement about this or that philosopher? How does it happen that we say yes to one philosopher and no to another one? We cannot demonstrate the factual truths of the philosopher that we like. It is not a problem of truth. The choice is based on sympathy (the sharing of a pathos), not on logical decision.

I feel aversion to Schopenhauer because I link the content of his thought (whose greatness I acknowledge) with the emotional vibration of this thought. His thought is the expression of a thinking body (as always, of course), the uttering of a pulsating singularity that is projected into a world of thought. My aversion is not to his thought, but to the existential singularity that is vibrating within his thought: the identification with the father, the resentment against motherly dissipation, the basic misogyny of his experience and of his *Weltanschauung*, and the reactionary hatred against rebels who do not respect the established order.

Schopenhauer, in my opinion, is the starting point of the history of a sort of *ubermenschlickheit* that is grounded on bitterness and hysterical claim (or melancholic nostalgia) of a potency that is vanishing.

Schopenhauer announced and resented the decline of male domination and that of the white race. Today this double decline is fully exposed: the human project must free itself from this identification with male potency.

The potency is over, the possibility is concealed. What we need is not the affirmation of a will, but the disentanglement of a possibility inscribed in the present composition of the world.

The Prince, the Fortune, the Virtue

Misogyny is implied in the history of humanism, and mostly in the late modern crisis of humanism. Think again: what is humanism? This time my answer will start at paragraph XXV of Niccolò Machiavelli's *The Prince*, titled 'Quantum Fortuna in Rebus Humanis possit, et quomodo illi sit occurrendum'.

Here the Florentine defines the relation between fortune and virtue, the chaotic occurrence of events and the regulating power of human action. 'I will compare Fortune to one of those ruinous rivers that rage and invade the empty spaces and destroy trees and buildings . . . So too does fortune: it shows its potency where ordered virtue does not resist it.'[4]

The word 'virtue' here refers to the ability of the Prince to govern the chaotic events labelled 'fortune' and to subjugate them to the will of power.

The Prince has to predict the direction of events, their force and destructivity, and most of all he must be energetic in order to submit fortune to his domination. He is not allowed to be respectful or hesitant, as he must impose his will through violence.

At the end of the same paragraph Machiavelli suggests a metaphor that contains, in my opinion, the deepest meaning of the modern conception of political power:

> I conclude that men are happy when they are in concord, while they
> are unhappy when they are in disagreement. Therefore, I assess that
> it is better to be forceful than respectful. In fact, Fortune is female,
> and if we want to subjugate her it is required to beat her and to hurt
> her. Actually, she prefers to be conquered by those who coldly
> proceed. Being a woman she is more friendly to young men who are
> not respectful and more audaciously prevail.[5]

The history of modern politics and civilization intended as the imposition of a technological order is here sketched: the Machiavellian definition of power is based on the distinction between feminine (the chaotic and capricious proliferation of possible events, potentialities rushing out of the depths of nature), and masculine will that imposes order on the flow, subjecting the flow to the rule of discrimination.

Potency is will that subjugates the possible and reduces it to order. This potency, then, is masculine, while the magmatic sphere of possibility is feminine. So, it is in Machiavelli's thought, and so, too, in the historical enactment of power.

The tools that the Prince must master are of a moral kind – cruelty, pitilessness, violence, resolution – but also of a technical kind: Machiavelli was, in fact, interested in military technologies. Such machines are the most important instrument of war, of the economy and of political power. In late modernity, however, technology exceeds the political sphere up to the point that technology has become the master of potency, replacing political will and reducing men to impotence.

Technique, Declining Male Potency and Reactionary Nostalgia

In *Letter on Humanism*, Heidegger writes that humanism is rising in the desert of being, i.e., in the space that opens when the ontological reduction of existence dissolves. We can speak of humanism when the elaboration of being happens in the sphere of language, and therefore language turns out to be the space and the limit of being.

When language becomes the language of technique (in the sense that technique turns out to be the subject of language), humans are expropriated of language; what is enforced on them is a chain of technical implications. When language undergoes the process of automation then it is the twilight of the humanist culture.

Heidegger seems unable to understand that technique is not a monolithic, unambiguous system, but the space in which technologies take shape in their ever-changing relation to strategy, political intention and social interest. Hence a reactionary nostalgia ensues, one whose idol is the world of authenticity that preceded the technological transformation. The nostalgia for authenticity is linked to the depressing perception of the decline of the West as a sort of counterbalance to progressive expectations of modern historical philosophy and positivism. This line of thought may be read as a presentation of the decline of the masculine potency that supported the energy of modernity.

The process of modernization is based on economic competition and military aggression. For instance, look to the role of Futurist culture in the process of Italian modernization: Futurism (and fascism, by the way) is an effort in masculinizing the collective self-perception of the nation. In order to gather economic and political force, in order to win wars and market competition, nations must remove the feminine side of their own culture. But the energy that supported nationalism and modernization at the beginning of the twentieth century is now over. Economic growth is receding, expansion collides against the physical limits of the planet, and global demographics point towards senility.

Potency had been conceived of in terms of penetration and subjection. In the late modern era, however, potency was doomed to give way to a system of technical devices which are better endowed than man to accomplish the goal of penetrating and subjugating fortune and the magma of events. Technique was born as the prosthesis of masculine penetrative potency, and at the end of the modern path the prosthesis takes the place of the organ itself, while the complexity and rising autonomy of the *Lebenswelt*, feminine world of unpredictable chaos and natural dissipation, is escaping the grip of order and domination.

After accomplishing the task of subjugating the natural world, men realize they have been expropriated of their potency as it has been absorbed and overwhelmed by technology.

From Schopenhauer to Nietzsche to Heidegger, there is a thread that may be identified as *Ubermenschlichkheit* nostalgia that is often (but not always) linked with reactionary right-wing politics. This crowd reacts to the painful consciousness of declining potency with masculine bitterness, and with an anti-feminine aggression that is increasingly marking daily life and international politics. The ongoing war that fanatic Islamists are waging against women is the most appalling demonstration of this anti-feminine hatred in the wake of the loss of male power, a symptom of the fearful perception of lessening potency of men in comparison with the rising potency of technique.

Dostoyevsky

As male frustration caused by the growing autonomy of women meets often with exalted religious spiritualism and sometimes with depression, male hysteria has flourished in literature.

In an essay published in 1921, Nikolai Berdyaev argues that Dostoyevsky has deeply investigated apocalypse and nihilism, exposing the metaphysical hysteria of the mythological Russian soul and its tendency to fall into obsession. This hysterical thread of the Russian psychology shows in authoritarian political forms, because only in Christ is freedom perfect. When freedom becomes mundane, the utopia of happiness and social perfection destroys inner freedom.

Berdyaev was conscious of the relation between this reactionary hysteria and an atrophy of emotionality, particularly
of the erotic perceptions of the body. In Dostoyevsky,
women do not exist as independent individuals. The human
soul is a manly business. 'Never in Dostoyevsky is love
described as something desirable, and no womanly character
holds independent meaning. Always it is the tragic manly
destiny impending. Women are only an interior tragedy of
men.'⁶

The same might be said about Nietzsche, if I get it right.
I'm hesitant and doubtful when I think about Nietzsche
because I do not understand his words, his intentions, his
philosophical project. I had a crush on him, once upon a
time, while reading a book by Deleuze (*Nietzsche and
Philosophy*, 1962).

'What a will wants is to assert its difference', writes
Deleuze as an introduction to Nietzsche. Instead of the
Hegelian 'work of the negation', the Deleuzian Nietzsche
preaches lightness and dancing. Persuaded by Deleuze's
words on Nietzsche, I undertook the difficult task of reading
some of his books myself (*On the Genealogy of Morals*, *The
Dawn*, *Ecce Homo*, *Schopenhauer as Educator* and *Thus Spoke
Zarathustra*).

Soon, I was wondering: why is this guy so nervous?
Why is he on such bad terms with professors, while a
professor himself? Why is he on such bad terms with
priests? Why is he on such bad terms with girls? That's
okay, it's not my business, but at the end I felt uneasy with
all his rhetoric about will, potency and force, coming from
a person so frail.

I don't care much about Nietzsche. I like him better than

Schopenhauer and Heidegger: he has the courage to disclose his own frailty and expose his mind to the tempests gathered by his own words, while the others evoke storms then retreat into a comfortable greedy refuge. I would not like to be friends with Schopenhauer, nor – for no reason – friends with Heidegger. Nietzsche could be a good friend – if perhaps a little bit pathetic. Nietzsche I like because he is irresponsible, light and crazy, but all the heroism and negative theology emanating from his books sound like parody, mimicking in anticipation the tragedy of the twentieth century.

With an acrobatic jump, we land in the age of hyper-connectivity and *hikikomori*. The body of the connective generation is stiffening in loneliness, like Schopenhauer's body, but simultaneously deploys itself in euphoric games of competition. The general intellect lives in the abstract dimension of connection, but the individual bodies of the cognitive workers are frail and fragmented by isolation. Like Schopenhauer, I'm looking for the living body of the networked *ich denke*, the living body that makes knowledge and production possible. But the body of Schopenhauer is unhappy, ceaselessly attracted by illusions that cannot enter into contact with the skin.

The Mother and the Sadness of the Flesh

Though loneliness is his main subject, Michel Houellebecq is not an intimist writer: the tangible pain that he is speaking of is not only his personal pain, but also the lens through which he looks at our age.

As he explains on his website, Houellebecq's parents lost

interest in him when he was six years old. He spent his childhood with his paternal grandmother, Henriette Houellebecq, whose name he later adopted. He studied agricultural science in Paris, began a career as a researcher, then was employed as a computer programmer, and fell into depression. 'Mine was the point of view of a depressed person, but I was not sad. I was idle,' he declared in an interview with an Italian newspaper in 2001.

I don't intend to psychoanalyze Michel Houellebecq from these declarations, and I'm not interested in the degree of autobiography that can be found in his novels. I'm interested in what his characters and his poetic world reveal of the present.

When I read *The Elementary Particles* (1998 [2006]), I immediately felt that Michel Houellebecq was expressing something deeply entrenched in our contemporary psychoscape, directly influencing our social and political behaviour. In the novel, two brothers, Michel and Bruno, live in a condition insulated from the history of their time. They appear like monastics, without windows on the world, as their ability to perceive the world around them had not been activated by the bodily contact of a human being during their early years. One of them (Michel) is a biologist who perceives the world as the sphere in which elementary particles recombine in a process of slimy composition and decomposition. The other one (Bruno) teaches in a high school and is sexually stunted, convinced that his penis is too small and inept. He has an occasional lover he meets in silent embarrassment, and he cannot stop himself from putting his hands on the thighs of young girls at the school.

For the brothers, the surrounding environment has no history; the bodies around them are not recognizable as conscious bodies because they, too, have no history, only depressing biology. Pleasure is not part of the possible experience of life. Only the spasm of wet mucous membranes and the spurt of organic liquids, the contraction of muscles, shameful excitement, and unmentionable discharge.

The origin of this sadness is to be found in the childhood of Bruno and Michel, and in their relation with a mother who never appears in the novel, because many years earlier she flew away with her Californian lover, leaving her children alone. The fierce anti-feminism of Houellebecq is already contained within this mother, a beautiful, sensuous Mediterranean-looking mother. The writer is explicitly linking the absence of the body of the mother and the sadness that haunts the sexualities and lives of Bruno and Michel.

> If the fundamental aspects of sexual behaviour are innate, the history of the first years of life is particularly important in the dynamics of its expression. Among birds and mammals, precocious skin contact with other members of the species seems vital . . . The deprivation of skin contact with the mother during early childhood results in serious perturbations of sexual behaviour of the mouse.[7]

Houellebecq imagines a world in which contact with the mother has been more or less precluded. For the writer, feminism and the hippy movement are guilty of this preclusion. While being a wonderful writer, Houellebecq, in fact, understands almost nothing of the cultural history of the last fifty years, up to the point that he identifies feminism with the working socialization of women (he is not alone in this misunderstanding). Actually, feminism has been such a complex and rich cultural experience that it is quite impossible to reduce it to a univocal definition, but the capture of women's time and sensibility by the capitalist machine was certainly not the main goal of feminists.

On the contrary, we may say that feminism is rather a glorification of sensuousness and laziness as a condition of happy socialization. Emancipationist feminism reclaims and obtains the access of women into the world of labour, the integration of the bodily (and mental) energies of women in the rhythm of production. The consequence has been the rarefaction of the mental and physical availability of the mother and the loneliness of children.

In the first connective generation, a social inability for happiness is spreading, an autistic tendency, a paralysis of empathy.

The resentful philosophy of Houellebecq is based on the assumption that the selfish '68 generation has consumed all the available pleasure, leaving nothing to the those who have come after. Of course, this reasoning is based on a huge misunderstanding, but I'm not writing to redress his ideas nor am I his psychoanalyst. I read Houellebecq because I want to see the world through his eyes. I don't ask writers to confirm my ideas; I ask them to help me to see the world through the eyes of someone else, as the world is the point of dynamic intersection of uncountable different outlooks. And the outlook of a writer (of a great writer as Houellebecq is, in my humble opinion) is a way to enhance our own understanding of the world.

The author of *The Elementary Particles* has the courage of despair, the courage to stare the beast in the eyes, to look into the genesis of contemporary fascism that springs from the loneliness of the male body, despicable and despised, and therefore aggressive. This book breaks apart the idealism of modern political culture, the hypocritical idealism of men who erect altars to the values of labour and homeland and war and land and blood because they know little about sensuality and conversation among conscious bodies.

Hatred for women and hatred for '68 culture, these are the repeated threads of Houellebecq's work. Nevertheless, I think he is one of the most important authors of our time, as he opens a window on the psychosphere of the age in which we are living. I think Houellebecq understands nothing of the culture of movements, and the social history of our time, but I'm not interested in what he thinks of the world. I'm interested in the world that he makes visible for me, the world as he perceives it, the world that he is projecting, because it is part of the (despairing and sad) world in which we dwell.

The personal pain of Houellebecq is not my business. What's interesting to me is the way he recounts the pain of the generation that emerged too late for the happy togetherness of bodies and minds, and too soon for full abstraction in the virtual emotional sphere.

We cannot ask writers to tell us the truth, because each writer is telling her own singular truth, her personal indignation transformed into universal indignation, her joy that enlightens the world in a singular way.

Of importance is the breadth of vision that an author opens to us, how large is the window she provides. The window given us by Houellebecq is very wide as he exposes some of the deepest currents of the contemporary zeitgeist, of the impending barbarity, of the irreversible devastation that is taking control of the psychosphere, and looms on the historical scene.

His latest novel, *Submission*, has been received with some scepticism. Many say that the plot is unbelievable. Others say that his predictions are too dark. He answered these remarks in the novel, reminding us that Cassandra's predictions were never believed, but always true.

The history that Houellebecq is unfolding is an unlikely one: it is indeed unlikely that an Islamic party would win the presidency of France. But its poetry is not in describing what is likely, but rather in revealing nightmares and illusions: it is in this way (that is, in the matter of the imagination) that the history of the world is created. This novel envisions the future of Europe from the point of view of the unconscious: the Europe of 11 January 2015, when a huge trompe l'oeil was projected onto the global mediascape. On that day, following the murders at the *Charlie Hebdo* offices, the *intra muros* Parisians (four million people who live in the city) marched to exorcize the fears of the *extra muros* Parisians (five million people who live, more or less, in the *banlieue*).

The massacre of 13 November 2015 at the Bataclan theatre has deepened the perception of an unbridgeable hatred prepared by two centuries of colonialism and by the last fifteen years of war. Westerners have been bombing Iraq, Afghanistan and Libya for years. Now that violence has produced a monster bombing Western cities. Will we overcome this nightmare? Presently it's hard to expect a positive outcome. Hundreds of thousands of migrants are fleeing the lands destroyed by Western aggressions, trying to reach Northern Europe in vain: they find walls and barbed wire.

From this huge crowd of despairing people, the next monster may arise to haunt the good people of Europe.

Submission and European Depression

Do you remember *La haine* (1995), the movie written and directed by Mathieu Kassovitz in which, one night, a group of black African and Arab youth emerge from their jungle-*banlieues* and go to the other world, the centre of Paris that is in reality only some metro stops away? In that movie you can find all the ingredients that combined to create the *Charlie Hebdo* rampage and the horrible massacre at the Bataclan theatre.

Most of the words written in the Western press in the days following those crimes were about defending free speech and freedom of the press. But this violence is not about free speech: it is about hatred and fear; it's about marginalization and violence.

Some of the Islamist killers have declared to the media that their murderous projects are rooted in the images from Abu Ghraib. Chérif Kouachi, one of the murderers in the attack in January, said that he started thinking about becoming a terrorist in the aftermath of that shock. His religious conversion came after, not before, the vision of that humiliation.

I remember what I thought in 2004, when I saw those photos taken by American soldiers. I thought: in this very moment, millions of Arab children are watching TV. They will wait until they are twenty years old, then they will devote their lives to beheading Westerners. Here we are: those children today are twenty years old, they have no expectation of social integration, and they live in an environment in which, every day, advertisements repeat that only if you win do you have a right to exist. Not surprisingly they want to be part of an Islamist army: Daesh gives them a salary of $400 a month that they will never get in London or Cairo, and they hope to kill a Westerner.

A group of true freedom defenders led the march in Paris on 11 January 2015. There was Viktor Orbán, who as prime minister is silencing the press and the media in Hungary. There was Ahmet Davutoğlu, prime minister of the Turkish Republic, who jails actors in movies that the regime does not like, and backs Daesh in order to aggress against the Kurdish people. There was Mohammed bin Ismail Al-Sheikh, the Saudi ambassador, whose democratic sensibility and respect for civil rights is well known. There was the Israeli Netanyahu, who is leading the Jewish people towards fascism and permanent war. And finally, there was Jean-Claude Juncker, who is today engaged in cutting the European worker's salary, but was yesterday engaged in persuading the big corporations operating in Europe not to pay taxes to the Union, and to invest in the banks of his small country of Luxembourg.

The Paris massacre produced in the European political culture a paradoxical identitarian effect: nationalism against migrants is growing alongside rage against the financial aggression that is impoverishing society.

European identity was based once upon a time on prosperity as a shared value. Economic security and social democracy were the *differentia specifica* of Europe, but financial aggression has transformed the Union into a machine of impoverishment.

In order to survive, the Union now needs a new identity.

Will it be the national-Europeanism that is rising in the form of nationalism, racism and resentment on the continent?

Submission narrates the process of the Islamization of the West, a paranoid phantasy that dwells within the European unconscious. One that persuaded the Norwegian Anders Breivik to kill seventy-seven young people. Obviously, there is no Islamization process in the West. There is a war spreading from Ukraine, from the Middle East, from Northern Africa. Europe is slowly (or not so slowly) sinking into it.

If we want to read the book as a political prophecy, it does not fit. It's about France governed by an Islamic party, and about parties where women are totally absent (can you imagine such a thing in Paris?). It's about the Sorbonne financed and directed by Saudi Arabia, and professors obliged to convert to Islam. Unrealistic.

But this is not the point. Philip K. Dick's plots are often scarcely credible when it comes to geopolitics, but he focuses instead on something more essential. So, too, does Houellebecq want to focus on something more important than the political destiny of the *Republique française*: he focuses on the European depression. At the origin of this depression lies, in my opinion, a sense of self-hatred, that is also at the core of the poetics of Houellebecq. Not fear but depression is the negative force feeding the aggressive identitarianism of European people. The same is true of the aggressive identitarianism of the Islamic world, of course.

The depression of Houellebecq does not have the romantic features of melancholy, it does not resound with the sublime of Novalis, and is not attracted by the sweet panic of the infinite. The contemporary sadness that Houellebecq depicts is a sordid sadness that springs from the dissolution of sympathy of human for human, resulting in uneasy sexual compulsion, or autistic repulsion of the body reduced to organic matter.

Houellebecq goes to the tangled heart of the contemporary depression, then he picks apart the knot, turning it into praise (well conceived, in philosophical terms) of submission. In the novel, submission is the cultural, psychological and therefore political force that makes Islam so strong that it can conquer Europe.

Islam accepts the world as it is, in the sense of Nietzsche. While Buddhists think that the world is *dukkha*, pain and imbalance, while Christians think that Satan is the lord of this world, for Islam the Creation is absolutely perfect, an absolute masterpiece. This is what the Islamized Dean of the Islamized Sorbonne says, in order to persuade the novel's protagonist.

In the chaotic universal nothingness, submission is seen as the only condition for the soul's peace, and also as the only condition for success.

In fact, submission to supreme law (the law of Allah or the law of the market) does not exclude, rather it implies, the subjugation of man to man, and particularly the subjugation of women.

Submission and Computability

A peculiar version of submission is at the core of techno-hype.

To understand the implications of digital submission, I'll refer to Kevin Kelly, one of the most important thinkers of

Californian digital-philosophy. After publishing the magazine *CoEvolution* in the '90s, Kelly became executive editor of the world-renowned magazine *WIRED*.

In 1993, a year that was crucial in the history of the creation of the Internet, he published a book called *Out of Control*. The core of this book was his assertion that the global mind, concatenation of machines and minds and eyes and software and more, is superior to the sub-global minds, and therefore we cannot understand, let alone judge or refuse, the rationale of the global network.

According to Kelly, the global mind's deployment has to be considered a process that we cannot affect or deviate, because we are at a level of knowledge that is under the law of the digital whole, and the expansion of the digital net is expanding the sphere of computation and reducing more spaces of life to the computational paradigm.

The final jump beyond the human condition will be inevitably provoked by the spread of artificially intelligent machines, disseminating themselves in the very fabric of daily life and of labour: 'The arrival of artificial thinking accelerates all the other disruptions . . . it is the ur-force of the future. We can say with certainty that cognification is inevitable, because it is already here.'[8]

Like the Islamist bowing to the inevitable inscribed in the mind of God, this religious vision of the techno-future leads Kelly to promote submission to the superior and unquestionable will of the networking machine.

But the machine has no will in and of itself, and the direction that the machine follows is the direction that the human creator had inscribed in it at a certain point in its historical evolution. This direction has been inscribed in such a form that it is acting as a gestalt that became unavoidable when it was turned into a tangle, but human consciousness is able to disentangle the mental activity from the limits and the traps of the gestalt.

There is a flaw in Kevin Kelly's philosophical description: he thinks that computation is going to penetrate into all the recesses of human life, language and behaviour. But this is not taking into consideration the incomputable: the vibrational, indeterminable quantum leaps that are inscribed in social behaviour and in linguistic excess.

Kelly does not account for the irreducibility of meaning to the measure of computability. However, in order to start a process of disentanglement and of re-formulation of the basic gestalt, we have to consider the force of the incomputable. The incomputable is the leading force of human evolution. This is why our history is human.

Comparing Leibniz and Don Quixote, in his book *The Universal Computer*, the mathematician Martin Davis sets Don Quixote's consciousness of worldly imperfection in opposition to Leibniz's idea that God has constructed the best possible world. 'Leibniz spoke of a universal artificial mathematical language in which each facet of knowledge could be expressed, of calculational rules which would reveal all the logical interrelationships among these propositions. Finally, he dreamed of machines capable of carrying out calculations, freeing the mind for creative thought.'[9]

But the theoretical premise of Leibniz is the radical reducibility of all phenomena of the world to a recombination of computable elements: 'God from his omniscient view of all possible worlds, had unerringly created the best that could be constructed, that all the evil elements of our world were balanced by good in an optimal manner.'[10] Davis, however, observes that this reduction is false. Even Leibniz himself was obliged to recognize that life and social involvement exposed the imperfection and approximation of the living organism, particularly of the consciousness of the living organism.

The perfection of the machine is the reason for its inadequacy to encompass the full infinity of imperfection.

Humanism and Theology

Houellebecq's ideological enemy is humanism. 'The word "humanism" makes me slightly sick', says the main character in *Submission*.

But what does he mean by this word?

For me, the word 'humanism' refers to the ontological indeterminacy of human action, to the independence of historical destiny from any theological principle.

For me, humanism is the negation of any theology, not only of traditional religious theologies, but also the economic theology based on the assumption that 'There Is No Alternative'.

At the beginning of the philosophical movement called humanism, Pico della Mirandola, in the *Oration on the Dignity of Man*, kindly invites God to leave the place, then gives men the anxiogenic thrill of a non-written destiny.

The depressed professor of Houellebecq's novel, for his part, despises humanism because, for him, the human can only be reduced to the biological, pulsional drive. He misses altogether the cultural genesis of desire: humanist freedom is consciousness, imagination, linguistic construction in the absence of ontological foundations.

This is the dimension in which modern adventure occurs: it is only secondarily about political freedom; primarily, it is about ontological indeterminacy, autonomy from Being.

The marriage of technique and the economy has generated the conditions for a new theocracy. The global machine of the market is the implicit destiny of men in the present post-humanist age. God is back, under the guise of technique. And Islam is only the complement to this neoliberal submission.

The Islamization that is described by Houellebecq is neoliberalism plus sharia. It is the moderate Islam that Western journalists are so fond of, the same one the Muslim Brotherhood has tried to build in Egypt, the same one of the Saudi petro-plutocracy. A double theocracy: Islamic, but respectful of the neoliberal theocracy. When the Islamic party has taken control in the France imagined by Houellebecq, its leader, Muhammad Ben Abbes aims to achieve the final liquidation of public expense and full privatization. The educational system is partly Islamic, financed by the Saudis, and partly private.

Reading *Submission*, one gets the impression that the author's predictions cannot be taken seriously as they are unimaginable, unlikely, impossible. This is what I thought myself, but I was wrong.

Ten years ago, it would have been impossible to image what has happened in Europe over the last five years. We could not have imagined that a country like Greece would be reduced to its present condition of misery and despair. We could not have imagined that one quarter of the Italian industrial system would be dismantled. We could not have imagined that European governments would resort to anti-migrant racism, or that nationalist parties would seize political power in so many countries. We could not have imagined that the Union would be destined to belie its fundamental values. We could not have imagined such a future as the one we are now living in. But in the end, such a future was possible, and has, in fact, come true. The theocratic folly of financial capitalism has made possible what could never before have been imagined.

3

The Dark Side of Desire

Ageing, Aesthetics and Politics

'Squaring the Pyramid of Ageing' is the title of an issue of the American magazine *Daedalus* (*Journal for the American Arts and Sciences*), published in the year 1980. The pyramid squares because people are living longer and the birth rate is declining: there are ever fewer young people and ever more elderly.

Some decades ago, those aged over sixty were a small minority. Sometimes they were surrounded by an aura of respect and veneration; more often they were rejected to the margins of society, deprived of the means for survival, unable to become a community. Now the circumstances are different: because of the declining birth rate and the prolongation of the average lifespan, the elderly are a relevant part of the overall population. As the heirs of the welfare decades, they have a regular pension and their opinion is important as they vote in massive numbers.

Nevertheless, the cultural significance of ageing is ignored, or reduced simply to the notion of decline.

What does the general trend towards senescence imply from a cultural or psychological point of view?

Western culture has always been obsessed with the foundational mythology of youthful energy. Not only sex, but also politics, arts, beauty all worship the cult of energy. 'Energy is Eternal Delight', as in the words of William Blake.

The fundamental energolatria of modern culture is shaken, frightened, and reacts defensively by displacing energy from the body to the technique. Senescent humans hand over their energy to the mechanical or chemical prosthesis, and invest in money as a substitute for bodily vigour.

In the family of the past century, the parents, thirty or forty years old, were the wealthy persons of the family. Now the forty-year-olds are precarious workers, unemployed, and no longer wealthy. Only sixty- and seventy-year-old grandparents have a regular pension, and it has become their turn to pay for the schooling of their nephews.

Those who were workers in the age of welfare are not now rich, but they do have some money every month, whereas the majority of the post-welfare workers are precarious and poorly paid. The market, as a result, is going to pay a special attention to the elderly. We need to elaborate theoretically and aesthetically on this demographic change, as well as its psychological and cultural implications and consequences.

Both the culture of the ruling class and the culture of movements have been shaped by the fundamental mythology of energy. Both commercial advertising and revolutionary propaganda are based on the energy of desire.

In their late work *What Is Philosophy?*, Deleuze and Guattari reconsider desire from the point of view of ageing. After a discussion of ageing and of friendship in the conclusion of the book, subtitled 'From Chaos to the Brain', they say that at a certain moment one perceives the suffering of the universe, chaos, and the surrounding acceleration that blurs perception, attention and understanding. The universe is too fast for the aged brain to elaborate it. This is the dark side of desire: the technical world that we have created in an age of youthful energy is now too fast and too complex for the human mind to control.

In his last book, *Chaosmosis*, Guattari speaks of the chaosmic spasm: the perception that we are no longer able to follow the rhythm of chaosmotic desire.

Physical, affective and historical events are slowing the pace of the brain as mind, and in the dissonance between the speed of the world and the slowness of the mind there is a suffering, which is the dark side of desire. But desire is not only energy and speed. It's also the ability to find another rhythm.

Here I am not only contemplating a problem of ageing, I'm talking about the art of politics, about the art of changing our conceptual frame.

We must abandon the point of view of productivity, the expectation of acquisition and of control. We must assume, instead, the point of view of laziness and self-care. We must transform impotence into a line of flight away from the universe of competition.

We may discover that being exhausted is not so bad.

How do we deal with the problem of exhaustion? Inscribing the reality of death in the political agenda. Transforming decline into a lifestyle of solidarity.

The senile generation of Europe may become the subject of a cultural revolution aimed to prepare Western society for a redistribution of wealth and resources. Such a cultural revolution should start with a critique of the cult of energetic youth that permeates modern culture. The ideology of unbounded growth and aggressive competition has underpinned the two pillars of capitalist development; they have nourished the romantic and nationalist ideologies that have aggressively mobilized Western society in late modern times.

We need a senile approach to the problem of the future. The cult of competition must be replaced by the cult of solidarity and of sharing.

I concede that this prospect seems very unlikely at present. The European population seems determined to defend its privilege with all the means at its disposal. However, this stance cannot bring anything good with it and is already bringing a lot of evil.

Young people escaping hard conditions are surrounding Fortress Europe. They bear with them the unconscious memory of centuries of exploitation and humiliation, as well as the conscious expectation of those things that advertising and global ideology have lately promised them.

Over the past decades, Europe seemed the continent of peace and social justice. Now it is sinking under a wave of sadness and cynicism. Young people seem unable to alter the social conditions and are wandering in a social labyrinth devoid of solidarity or peace.

The senile population could, then, be the bearer of a new hope, if they are able to face the inevitable with an easy soul. They may discover something that humankind has never known: the love of the aged, the sensuous slowness of those who no longer expect any good to come from life except wisdom. This is the wisdom of those who have seen much, forgotten nothing, but still look at everything with innocent curiosity.

The Message of Francis

In *Habemus Papam* (*We Have a Pope*, 2011) (this director's best movie, in my opinion), Nanni Moretti portrays the impotence of human beings facing the immensity of historical suffering. God is nowhere in the movie, and the newly elected pope, played by Michel Piccoli, feels unable to express with words the unimaginable chaos of reality in the absence of God.

The genius of Nanni Moretti foretold a drama that unfolded in the Church of Rome just a few months after the release of the movie.

In February 2013, Joseph Ratzinger, the German pope who asserted the unquestionable superiority of truth against any relativism, resigned, declaring his physical and spiritual feebleness. This was an act of unprecedented courage and humility that we should interpret in philosophical terms as an acknowledgement of the political impotence of ethical reason.

I'm not a theologian and I don't pretend to deeply understand the meaning and intentions behind such an enormous act. However, from the point of view of secular philosophy, I claim that the resignation of Ratzinger, or Pope Benedict XVI, marked the failure of the historical attempt to master and subdue the unchained forces of evil, as materialized in the animal instincts of global capitalism. Overwhelmed by his own weakness, Benedict fell silent and bowed his head. Admitting his own impotence was in my view the highest sign of his fortitude.

Then something else happened. In a time when sectarian violence, conservative arrogance, and economic greed have taken the upper hand almost everywhere, a new man appeared at the window of Saint Peter's Basilica and hailed the crowds with a simple, 'Good evening.'

I'm not a believer, and my atheism makes it difficult for me to accept the idea that the Holy Spirit enlightened the high clergy who met in the papal conclave over those days in March 2013. However, human wisdom, at least, led them to elect a new pope, Pope Francis, who seems to stand – alone – against ethnic violence, political oppression and economic exploitation.

I cannot pretend to adequately interpret the theological significance of Pope Francis's preaching, nor do I intend to. But I do want to understand the philosophical implications of his acts and his words from a historical perspective. On 11 April 2015, Francis released his *Misericordiae Vultus* to inaugurate a Holy Year of Mercy, and the document is an explicit redefinition of the relation between truth and compassion, insisting upon the superiority of compassion over truth.

We may replace the word 'compassion' here with the word 'empathy', also with the word 'solidarity'.

The Pope, who, in his own words says he came from 'the end of the world', has declared that the Church should be seen as a military field hospital:

> What the Church needs more today is the ability to heal the wounds, and to warm the heart of the believers, the proximity. I see the Church as a military field hospital. It's useless to ask a seriously wounded person if he has high cholesterol. His wounds have to be healed. Then we'll speak about other things. Healing wounds is our mission . . . and we must start from below.[1]

What is striking is the Pope's intellectual courage to abandon the discourse of hope. In doing so, he interprets the prevailing sentiment of our time: a hopeless perception of the future. However, he translates this hopelessness in terms of mercy, compassion and friendship.

In Christian parlance, without faith, hope is impossible. And faith seems to be over, since communism, democracy and social progress crumbled at the end of the last century. Only capitalism survives. But faith in capitalism has collapsed as well, in these years of financial arrogance and precarious work. In the 1990s, capitalism was proclaimed to be the universal and ultimate model of social life, conquering the minds, too, of many deficient left-wing intellectuals. Now, only twenty years later, capitalism has lost almost all of its credibility, but is ruling as an unstoppable automatic machine. It is no longer winning by the force of consent; it is subjugating souls and bodies by force.

So, faith is over.

I'm not a believer; I trust in no god and no ideology, so I don't think that the end of faith is a bad thing. On the contrary, I think that when we are freed from faith we can grasp the real tendency of the time, and we can seize the most interesting opportunities that the tendency brings about.

But in order to seize the possible and to actualize it, we need friendship, solidarity, happiness and the ability to take pleasure in physical relations. This is what we lack today. Not hope, not faith, but friendship is what is truly lacking. This is why humanity is teetering on the abyss of war and suicide.

My interpretation of the words of Francis may be read as blasphemous, but not incongruous with their intended meaning: God is not here to take care of our wars, our pollution, our exploitation or the precariousness of our work. He is possibly very busy with something more urgent – who knows. We have to make do without his help.

Consequently, we must abandon hope: the world machine is ungovernable, and human will is impotent. Only friendship is left. This is how I understand Pope Francis's words.

In a fascinating text titled 'Pope Franciscus Under a Bright Red Star', Federico Campagna compares the actions of the pope elected in 2013 with the actions of the pope elected in 1503: Julius II, the '"Pope dressed in armour," the warrior Pontifex who had spent his life fighting to "push back the barbarians."'

Campagna proposes a political interpretation of the message of Francis, the pope who summons social activists, and aims to become the reference point of that part of the world population that has no other political representation since the fall of the Communist Revolution.

As for me, I do not deny that Francis's preaching has political intentions and effects, but I don't think this is the man's most important message. The most important, in my humble opinion, is his suggestion that Christ did not come to Earth to impose justice, but to preach friendship and compassion – like Siddhartha Gautama, by the way, who similarly spoke of great compassion as the only way to harmonize the singularity of existence with the cosmic game.

On 10 September 1978, a Pope named Albino Luciani declared that 'God is more a mother than a father.' He died only a few weeks after issuing his scandalous affirmation.

By saying that Christ is more merciful love than severity of truth, Pope Francis is rephrasing Luciani's concept. By focussing his attention on mercy, he emphasizes God's motherly attention to the frailty of the human creature, over a fatherly obsession with the law.

Obviously, we must read this in political terms: Christians are murdered in many countries because of their religious beliefs. But Francis does not call for a crusade. On the contrary, he has repeatedly blamed Western powers for their aggressive behaviour against Islam.

We can read his emphasis on mercy in the context of financial violence and European austerity, both of which are destroying the lives and futures of the Greek people – and not only theirs. We can also read the pope's emphasis on mercy in relation to the selfishness of European countries who refuse to accept migrants fleeing countries like Syria, Iraq and Afghanistan, countries pushed into the abyss by infinite Western wars.

As I do not expect redemption in my afterlife, I think that despair is the only appropriate intellectual stance in this time. But I also think that despair and joy are not irreconcilable, as despair is the mood of the intellectual mind, while joy is the mood of the embodied mind. Friendship is the force that transforms despair into joy. This is the lesson that I learn from the man who came from the end of the world.

II
Power

In the second part of this book, I try to understand and to describe the contemporary transformations of power, intended as a reduction in the field of possibilities to a determinist structure.

What is the shape of political and economic power in our time?

Less and less can we identify power with human actors making decisions and enforcing their will; more and more with techno-semiotic chains of automation.

This automation of power is not, however, leading to the implementation of the imperial order, as was the dream of the Western leading class after 1989.

The project of imperial domination of the world has failed; terror and local wars are jeopardizing the G7 (or G8 or G20) conception of an international order. The separation of the social brain from the social body has provoked an explosion of centrifugal conflicts. Power is based simultaneously on automation and on terror.

Automation is the rule of abstraction embedded in the deployment of the connective brain, and terror is the effect of brainless actions. Countless conflicting actors who have lost any prospect of social recomposition and any rational political strategy end up resorting to the ultimate factor of identity: violence, aggression, war.

In this part, I'll describe power as a process of the construction of the cognitive automaton: the neurology of leafcutter ants is taken as an exemplification of the contemporary project of technological subjugation of the living brain. The financial economy and the evolving forms of money and code are seen as the fields of implementation of the cognitive automaton.

4

Automation and Terror

We cannot describe the historical process in terms of problems and solutions.

Problem solving only exists in the field of mathematics. In the human world, problems are not solvable as the process of healing is interminable. Problematic situations evolve, change the horizon, and finally disappear as new problematic situations emerge and take shape.

Social evolution can be described as the succession of insolvable conundrums, emerging possibilities, vibrational oscillations, and finally selection and enforcement of one possibility among many: a provisional solution that neither solves nor stabilizes the infinite complexity of the conjunctive life.

I call power the temporary condition of implementation of a selection among many possibilities. I call power a regime of visibility and invisibility: the exclusion of different possible concatenations from the space of visibility.

A form emerges from many possible forms, then it turns into a gestalt, a format of perception of the surrounding reality. The gestalt is a perceptual code: a form that generates forms.

This is power.

If we want to describe the political form that power is taking nowadays, we have to start with the effects of neoliberal globalization and digital technology in the structure of the world: the transition from industrial modernity to the present network of globalization has been conceptualized as the shift from the model that Foucault defined as the disciplinary subjection of socialized bodies to the model of control that Deleuze outlines in his article 'Postscript on the Societies of Control'.

'Control', Deleuze writes,

> is the name Burroughs proposes as a term for the new monster, one that Foucault recognises as our immediate future. Paul Virilio also is continually analysing the ultra-rapid forms of free-floating control that replaced the old disciplines operating in the time frame of a closed system. There is no need here to invoke the extraordinary pharmaceutical productions, the molecular engineering, the genetic manipulations, although these are slated to enter into the new process.[1]

Following the suggestion of William Burroughs, Deleuze identifies 'control society' as the pervasive embodiment of a principle of automation of behaviour that is replacing the old principle of obedience to an external order.

> As the corporation replaces the factory, perpetual training tends to replace the school, and continuous control to replace the examination. Which is the surest way of delivering the school over to the

corporation. In the disciplinary societies one was always starting again (from school to the barracks, from the barracks to the factory), while in the societies of control one is never finished with anything – the corporation, the educational system, the armed service being metastable states coexisting in one and the same modulation, like a universal system of deformation.[2]

If we want to describe the social form that power takes now, we have to recall Marx's distinction between formal domination and real domination in the relation between capital and work.

In a text that is known as the (unpublished) sixth chapter of *Capital*, Marx defines formal subsumption as a compulsive relation, whose aim is to extract surplus labour by prolonging labour time.

A few pages later Marx defines real subsumption:

The real subsumption of labour under capital is developed in all the forms which develop relative, as distinct from absolute, surplus value.

With the real subsumption of labour under capital there takes place a complete [and a constant, continuous, and repeated] revolution in the mode of production itself, in the productivity of labour and in the relation between capitalist and worker. In the case of the real subsumption of labour under capital, all the changes in the labour process itself actually take effect. Labour's social powers of production are developed, and with labour on a large scale the application of science and machinery to direct production takes place. On the one hand, the capitalist mode of production changes the shape of material production. On the other hand, this alteration of production's material shape forms the basis for the development of the

capital-relation, which in its adequate shape therefore corresponds to
a specific level of development of the productive powers of labour.[3]

In the dimension of formal subsumption, the labour process
is not changed, even if it is subjected to the economic domination of the capitalist. In order to increase relative surplus
value (the amount of surplus value produced in the unit of
time), the capitalist introduces technological changes in the
labour process so as to increase the intensity of exploitation
and finally the amount of surplus value. This transformation
marks the passage from formal to real subsumption. In the
first phase the capitalist simply expropriates the work of the
product of his/her work. In the second phase the capitalist
transforms the labour process to intensify the rhythm of
production.

Real subsumption coincides with the introduction of
machines whose function is the intensification of labour
productivity, and the replacement of physical acts of material transformation. Automation is the ultimate form of
subsumption, as human time is automatically captured by
the flow.

Automation today is invading the very sphere of cognition (memory, learning and decision), so paving the way for
the ultimate form of subsumption: what I call 'mental
subsumption'. Power at this point takes the form of bio-
power, as it is embodied in the neuro fabric of social life
itself.

However, this process of the emergence of bio-power is
far from linear or uncontroversial. While technology
subsumes and reshapes the concatenation among brains in
the bunkered space of the digital network, the living body of

the planet inhabits the physical space that stretches outside of that bunker. This separation amounts to a loss of social consciousness, a dissolution of social solidarity and finally to a politics of belonging, aggression and war.

In the following pages, I will outline the forms that power takes in the present age: the inscription of automated patterns of language and interaction, on the one hand; the explosion of brainless forms of suicidal behaviour, on the other.

The Brisk Mutation

How long did it take, first, to inscribe the virus-language in the living space of Homo sapiens? How long did it take for linguistic mutation?

How many thousands of years have been necessary for language to become rooted and coherent enough to define the human race?

How long did it take, thereafter, before writing – as well as the technology able to transfer information, thought and emotion across space and time – was sufficiently established and disseminated to shape thought, communication, production and political power?

From the Code of Hammurabi to Gutenberg, we can count four thousand years. Language enabled the emergence of society, the differentiation of human beings from their environment, and enabled the jump beyond their existing reality that, according to Paolo Virno, was made possible through the faculty of negation. In the space of language, the double process of negation and imagination became possible.

In the passage from the twentieth to the twenty-first

century, we entered a new mutation, not less deep or full of implication than in the previous two mutations. This newest mutation is based on the capture, subsumption and integration of language into the digital network. The connective capture of those agents of signification that we call human beings has been deployed in the space of thirty, maybe fifty, years. In a very short span of time, everything has been unsettled: work, emotion, perception. The very modes of cognition have been shaken and reshaped. The memory, attention, intentionality and imagination of the generation born inside the Internet are so radically modified that the inter-generational interchange may be upset, disturbed, possibly deactivated.

The digital sphere is generating a cognitive mutation, a shift from the conjunctive to the connective mode of concatenation. We might call the new condition 'neo-human'.

I call 'conjunctive' a language mode in which the meaning of signs is grounded in the act of signification that happens in context. A language mode in which the rules of signification do not pre-exist signification, even if syntactic rules work in enunciation.

Conjunction is concatenation of irregular bodies that do not correspond to any prefabricated model, and do not act in accordance with an inscribed structure. Conjunctive bodies are not pre-formatted; they can choose the dimension in which linguistic exchange occurs, they can define in an aleatory way the level of the exchange, and they can displace this plan, they can break it, without respecting any syntactic order external to the signifying process of enunciation in context.

Connection displaces the process of signification from a

dimension in which conscious bodies conjoin according to aleatory patterns to a dimension in which bodies adapt to a code, to a digital format of exchange.

Conjunctive practices lose their pragmatic effectiveness, as the exchange of meaning presupposes compliance with the automated procedure of digital signification.

The behaviour of connective organisms (neo-humans) cannot be understood nor governed by the operational tools of politics, nor can they be judged by the moral categories inherited from the past age of humanism and critique, as these categories are linked to pre-connective patterns of cognition.

Neo-humans can process refined forms of interaction and store amounts of information incomparably superior to that which previous generations could store. But modalities of synthesis and elaboration follow lines that are not compatible with empathic consciousness.

In connective conditions, the interaction between neo-human units (organisms physically different but interconnected at the cognitive level) tends to be automated. Connective neo-humans tend to be more and more integrated through swarm behaviour.

Individual cognitive activity is increasingly connected to the meta-machine. Each individual is (or may be) sharply conscious of her own condition, but she is no longer able to govern it or change it, as the interaction is no longer dependent on ethical or political will but on the rules of the automaton.

Young precarious workers of the present generation are acutely conscious of the misery they are experiencing, of the exploitation they suffer and of the loneliness in which they are segregated. However, their communication is based on digital connection, less and less on the physical presence of the body of the other. They are no longer speaking their own language; they are spoken by it.

In 2015, the Oxford English Dictionary's Word of the Year was a pictograph: 😂, officially called the 'Face with Tears of Joy' emoji. The pictogram standardized by the machine is the main sign of human concatenation. We need less and less to express ourselves: a wide range of digital emoticons can express our feelings while advances in digital biometrics pave the way for emotion recognition.

What about self-perception? What about the emotional becoming?

How can the sentiment of impotence, mental suffering and ethical disease be reabsorbed, healed or at least cauterized?

By the word 'automaton' I do not mean a machine, but a super-individual bio-informatic organism that can traverse sensible singularities but cannot be traversed by them. The bio-info superorganism produces meaning by following rules that are compliant with the digital machine, and can act effectively only within the semiotic universe of connection.

The automaton takes the place of the sensitive, conscious individual organism able to pursue effective strategies of differentiation and transform its environment accordingly: this was the meaning of politics, in the sphere of alphabetical sequential communication.

The financial agent, on the contrary, produces effects only if his strategies comply with the strategy of the automaton.

Conjunctive enunciation cannot be effective in the sphere

of connective concatenation because it does not possess the code to access the technical syntax of the connective machine.

Only enunciations compatible with the connective logic can function and produce real effects. This is why the political will, and particularly the democratic process of decision, is unable to counter financial power. The relation between social life and the financial system is automated, inscribed in the technical network of governance.

The social body that rebels against the automaton is obliged to choose between impotence and suicide. Replaced by connective governance, the conjunctive body is reduced to impotence. Not surprisingly the suicide rate has been growing (60 per cent, according to the World Health Organization) over the last four decades. Not surprisingly, terrorist suicides are also spreading.

The Dissolving of the Masses

In his *Mass Psychology of Fascism*, Wilhelm Reich writes that the troubling question is not why people go on strike and revolt, but the other way around. Why do people not strike all the time? Why don't people rebel against oppression?

In our age, after the century marked by the rise and fall of the communist hope, we can choose from among many answers to this question.

People are unable and unwilling to revolt because they do not see the way to autonomy and solidarity because of the precariousness, anxiousness and competition that are linked to the present organization of work. Labour deterritorialization and technological fragmentation of the social body result in the inability to create effective networks of solidarity and in widespread loneliness broken only by sudden, random explosions of rage. This is one possible answer.

A second answer is the dissolution of the physical identity of power. Power is nowhere and everywhere at the same time, internalized and inscribed in the techno-linguistic automatisms called governance. Recent waves of rebellion have proven unable to focus their struggles against a physical centre of financial domination because a physical centre does not exist.

The precarization of labour, implying the end of territorial proximity and the widespread sentiment of anxious competition among workers, has provoked the dissolution of social solidarity that Jean Baudrillard predicted from the second half of the '70s.

In those years of transition from the industrial civilization to the digital civilization, a change occurred as well in the conceptual field and in the disciplinary organization of knowledge. This disciplinary reshuffling reflects the transformation that took place in the decades of neoliberal reformation and its intersection with digital technology.

Since the '80s the academic field of mass psychology has been replaced by a wide range of disciplines: sociology, psychology, cybernetic science, cultural studies and media theory. I don't want to investigate the academic motivations and implications of this disappearance and replacement; I want to focus on the real disappearance from the modern scene of the masses as a homogeneous body of social existence.

The masses are actually fading, almost vanishing. The emergence of the post-mass media technology for networked communication has dispelled the crowd, turning it into a sprawl of connecting atoms, while the precarization of labour disintegrates the physical proximity of workers. Social precarity can, indeed, be described as a condition in which workers are continuously changing their individual positions so that nobody will ever meet anybody in the same place twice. Cooperation without physical proximity is the condition of existential loneliness coupled with all-pervading productivity.

Workers do not perceive themselves anymore as parts of a living community: they are rather compelled to compete in a condition of loneliness. Although they are exploited in the same way by the same capitalist entity, they are no longer a social class because in their material condition they can no longer produce collective self-consciousness or the spontaneous solidarity of a community of people who live in the same place and share the same destiny. They are no more 'masses' because their random coming together in the subway, on the highway, or in similar places of transit is random and temporary.

Mass psychology is dissolving because the masses themselves are dissolving, at least in the social mind's self-perception. The concept of 'masses' is ambiguous and hard to define, as Baudrillard wrote in *In the Shadow of the Silent Majorities*, published at the end of the '70s.[4]

The concept of 'masses' diverges from the Marxist concept of 'social class', the aggregation of people who share interests, behaviour and consciousness. The existence of the working class is not an ontological truth: it is the effect of a shared imagination and consciousness. It is a mythology, in the strong sense of the world; a narration about the present and about the possible future. That narration vanished together with the social conditions of industrial production and with the end of the physical mass of workers in the space of factories. Over the last three decades, the cultural conditions for class self-perception have been negated by the post-industrial transformation of capitalism.

The dissolution of this massive dimension of society can be linked to the utter individualization and competitive disposition of workers in the age of precarization. 'Everything changes with the device of simulation: collapse of poles, orbital circulation of models (this is also the matrix of every implosive process).'

And he continues:

> Bombarded with stimuli, messages and texts, the masses are simply an opaque, blind stratum, like those clusters of stellar gas known only through analysis of their light spectrum – radiation spectrum equivalent to statistics and surveys – but precisely: it can no longer be a question of expression or representation, but only of the simulation of an ever inexpressible and unexpressed social.[5]

Whereas Guattari was attracted to the technological rhizome of information as a tool for liberation, Baudrillard expressed awareness of the dark side of the network: the dissipation of social energy, the implosion of subjectivity, the subjection of mental activity to the logic of simulation.

Guattari was interested in the concept of the network (*reseau*) because he saw in it a process of self-organization of social actors and the condition for a media-activist movement, but Baudrillard anticipated the effects of the new post-social power that was emerging under the umbrella of neoliberalism, taking the form of a network rather than the old form of the hierarchical pyramid.

Social autonomy and neoliberal deregulation are two simultaneous processes implying each other to some extent. The concept of the rhizome is a concept that maps the explosion of the hierarchical disciplinary society and the process of capitalist deregulation that paved the way for the precarization of work and the dissolution of social solidarity.

Thatcher and Baudrillard

Baudrillard wrote *In the Shadow of the Silent Majorities* in the same era when Margaret Thatcher was taking control of the Tory Party, beginning the triumphal progress that prepared her victory in the national elections of 1979, and launching the project that we have come to know as the neoliberal reformation. Echoing Baudrillard's concepts, in a 1987 interview Thatcher said:

> What irritated me about the whole direction of politics in the last thirty years is that it's always been towards the collectivist society. People have forgotten about personal security. And they say: do I count, do I matter? To which the short answer is, yes. And therefore, it isn't that I set out on economic policies; it's that I set out really to change the approach, and changing the economics is the means of changing that approach. If you change the approach you really are after the heart and soul of the nation. Economics are the method; the object is to change the heart and soul.[6]

The final goal of Thatcher's revolution was not economic, but political, ethical – almost spiritual, we might say. The neoliberal reformation was intended to inscribe competition into the very soul of social life, up to the point of destroying society itself. This cultural intention has been clearly described by Michel Foucault in his 1979–80 seminar published under the title *The Birth of Biopolitics*: the subjection of individual activity to the spirit of enterprise, the overall recoding of human activity in terms of economic rentability, the insertion of competition into the neural circuits of daily life. These are the trends that Foucault foresaw and described.

Not only economic profit, but moreover the cult of the individual as economic warrior, the harsh perception of the fundamental loneliness of humans, the cynical concession that war is the only possible relation among living organisms on the path of evolution: this is the ultimate intention of the neoliberal reformation.

Margaret Thatcher said, 'There is no such thing as society. There are individual men and women, and there are families. And no government can do anything except through people, and people must look to themselves first.'[7] The concept here is interesting but not accurate: society cannot disappear at the very end; sociability may be dissolving, but not society. Over the last thirty years, society has been transformed into a sort of blind system of inescapable obligation and interdependence, a prison-like condition of togetherness in which empathy is void and solidarity is forbidden.

The social space has been transformed into a worldwide system of automatic connections in which individuals cannot experience conjunction but only functional connection. The process of cooperation does not stop, it is transformed into a process of abstract recombination of info-fractals that only the code can decipher and transform into economic value. The mutual interaction is not negated outright, but empathy is replaced by competition. Social life proceeds, more frantic than ever: the living, conscious organism penetrated by dead, unconscious mathematical functions.

Will the Future Be American?

Empire, by Toni Negri and Michael Hardt, the most important theoretical book of the first decade of the new century, was based on the assumption of a fundamental isomorphism between the global order of the net and the order of the world.[8]

This assumption has been proven wrong: the world of life is held together by the digital net, while simultaneously exploding beyond the limits of the net itself.

In that book Negri and Hardt outlined the transition from a 'modern' phenomenon of imperialism, centred on individual nation states, to an emergent postmodern construct created among super-national and post-national ruling powers labelled 'empire'.

The history of the first fifteen years of this century has completely belied this thesis: the residual body of nationalism and of countless acentred conflicts is rotting at the borders of the imperial order of networked globalization, and the decay of the physical body of the planet has exceeded and overthrown the imperial attempt, proving that the concept of empire is only a utopia. This consideration is not intended to lessen the importance of the book, but to pave the way to a new understanding of the postmodern becoming of the world, based on the contradictory and complementary relation between automation and terror.

Contrary to the implicit assumption of *Empire*, the United States of America is no longer the global geopolitical master. The fragmented global civil war cannot be militarily controlled by the superpower.

Barack Obama has clearly understood and explained that US interventionism in Euro-Asian territory would be 'Doing Something Stupid'. After the Bush decade, the US geopolitical defeat is crystal clear, and the bombastic rhetoric of Donald Trump confirms this point. 'Make America Great Again' implies a renunciation of the imperial function, a fundamentally isolationist choice.

'America first' implies a declaration of rolling back from empire.

But America is not only a nation, or a political entity. It is also first and foremost a cultural process of trans-human metamorphosis, embodied in technology and culture.

As the political potency of the American nation declines irreversibly, the deterritorialized power of technology is transforming global behaviour, the global mind and the global unconscious. The engineers, futurists, scientists and entrepreneurs of the Global Silicon Valley are continuously transforming the mindscape of the planet. No roll-back will be possible at this level.

As a nation and as a military power, the United States of America will never regain its position of dominance that seemed unshakeable after the collapse of the Soviet empire. Does that mean that America is declining and the twenty-first century will not be American?

If we try to better define 'America', if we start from the

original decision of the Founding Fathers to displace the house of God from the old continent to the New-Found Land, we can acknowledge that 'America' is not the name of a territory but rather the name of a deterritorialization.

The Puritan imprint on American culture is not only a mark of religious dissidence from the history of European religious wars, it is also the project of purification of the future from the slag heaps of the past. Puritanism, indeed, is the name of the desire to create a new world in a space that is pure of history and culture, and distinct from reality itself: in this religious space, virtualization was conceived.

This is why America (and not the United States) is the future of the world.

America is the deterritorialized dimension of digital dis-identity. A virtual and recombinant dis-identity.

Desiring to be American while simultaneously hating the United States, is the paradox of many world populations.

Millions of people thus try to react against their own subaltern imagination: they cannot succeed because they are intimately colonized. The only way to stop the deterritorialized domination of America is to destroy the world itself: the political project of Islamic fundamentalism.

Cognitive automation or ultimate all-destroying war. Or both.

Decline of the Westphalian Order

In an interview released in the '90s, Zbigniew Brzezinski, former national security adviser in the Carter administration and prominent intellectual of the US establishment, said that the historical event of the collapse of the Soviet Union was incomparably more important than the rising of Islamist fanaticism.

Adopting the model of interpretation that was fit for the Cold War era, Brzezinski thought that the ultimate enemy of Western civilization was the centralized potency of the Soviet empire, which mirrored it at the military level but contained the seeds of an ideological alternative to capitalism. That model of interpretation was already out of order when the geopolitical West triumphed. Some months after, in fact, the first Gulf War opened a new asymmetrical dimension of conflict, and the Yugoslavian wars erupted: the bipolar scenario was replaced by a scenario of the proliferation of acentred conflicts.

After 1989, the US political and military hegemony appeared indisputable, but 11 September 2001 changed this view dramatically. Twenty-five years later, it's hard to claim that the US still has hegemonic potency

After winning the Cold War, the US lost all the hot wars the Bush administration chose to fight. George Bush II clearly entered his own suicidal drive after the suicidal aggression of al Qaeda. If we look at the results of fifteen years of an inexorable War on Terror, one may think that the strategic aim of Dick Cheney and George Bush was to sabotage American greatness. We should not, however, underestimate ignorance, pomposity and short-sightedness when trying to explain historical processes: ignorance, pomposity and short-sightedness led the Bush tribe into the trap set by bin Laden.

The colossal idiocy of the American ruling class resulted in the country's fantastic strategic self-annulment. Al Qaeda pushed that immense potency to turn against itself: the only way to destroy the hegemony of the United States. More than ten years later, surveying the political impotence of the Obama administration from beyond the grave, Osama bin Laden can legitimately say: mission accomplished.

The endless war launched by the Bush tribe has sent the enormous military force of the US in contradictory directions: entering the war between Sunni and Shiite, the US has strengthened one of its mortal enemies. Without joining the fight, the Iranian theocracy has emerged the winner of the Iraq War, and has gained control of Baghdad. When Americans armed the rebellion against Bashar al Assad, they helped jihadists lay the foundations of the Caliphate. And so on.

If we look at things from a geopolitical point of view, we can conclude that the US has defeated itself as a national potency.

However, America means more than a nation state. Thanks to the peculiarity of the creation of the North American State and to the cultural origin of technological innovation, America is essentially the anthropological dimension in which the post-territorial model of power is grounded.

In the American cultural space (by which I do not mean the territory of the US), digital technology, as an aesthetic and cognitive transformer, has turned into the main agent of world transformation.

This is why the future will likely be American, notwithstanding the strategic decline of the US potency.

The semio-corporations that embody the American cultural space are the actors of a post-earthbound history, while the Earth seems to be destined for increasing physical decay. The global corporations of semio-production are shaping the future beyond-Earth mindscape.

According to the geopolitical interpretation, the United States seems poised to decline, but the geopolitical criterion is absolutely insufficient to fully explain the deepest processes of this transformation.

The principle of national sovereignty established by the Westphalia Treaty is dissolving. From the Westphalia Treaty to the Congress of Vienna to the Treaty of Versailles, the political evolution of the modern world has been based on the steady assertion of the nation state, a juridical entity entitled to manage the flows of information, to issue currency and to control its territory with an army. Post-Westphalian potencies are surfacing: the Caliphate is poised to act as an attractor of the Islamist suicidal drive. Russia is poised to become the attractor of (anti-)European nationalist fronts.

In 1977, Simon Nora and Alain Minc (an engineer and a sociologist) in a report to the French president Valery Giscard d'Estaing, outlined a future of decay for national sovereignty. In their outlook, this decay was rooted in the loss of control of flows of information, and particularly of financial flows. In their report, titled *L'informatisation de la societé,* telematics (the connection of telephone and information technology) was designated the key to a post-national future.

In the decades that have followed its publication, the deterritorialization of monetary flows has provoked the loss of authority of the nation state in the financial field, while big corporations are managing volumes of capital much larger than most nation states do.

Furthermore, the globalization of the labour market has provoked the mobilization and displacement of hundreds of millions of people who are no longer under the jurisdiction of any nation state. Finally, military control of its territory is less and less a privilege of the nation state: private military agencies are taking control of wide swaths of the planet, while multinational armies like al Qaeda, Daesh and international narco-mafias have so much military power they can destroy the daily life of entire populations.

The geopolitical model of the nation state is no longer able to explain the daily business of life. A new model of interpretation is needed, and it must be based on the digital technological transformation.

Only, apparently the nation states are the holders of power: they control the territories, but the true actor of our time is digital abstraction, financial automatism and the process of automation of cognitive activity.

While subsuming the activity of the social brain, the financial market globalization and the online economy tend to displace power from the nation states to agencies of governance. Deterritorialized spheres of power are replacing the disempowered territorial agencies that sink in the global fragmentary war.

Less and less is the state the agent of social control. More and more, social control is incorporated in the biotechnical sphere. Neither politics nor military force can command the increasing complexity of life forms, social knowledge and productivity that are spreading in the networked world. Control must be transferred to the bodies themselves, to the relations among bodies. This is why we speak of bio-power.

The relations among individuals are wired and subjected to automatic connections: political power, therefore, is replaced by a system of techno-linguistic automatisms inclined towards the automation of every space of life, cognition and production.

Marx distinguished between formal domination and real domination: formal subsumption he defined as the brutal strength that forces individuals to accept exploitation in primordial conditions of absolute surplus value extraction. Thanks to the development of industrial machines enabling the increase of productivity and the extraction of relative surplus value, the system enters the regime of real subsumption: command is embodied in the machines and the act of subjugation is automated.

When we shift from the industrial to the informational machine, the regulation of the acts of production is no longer dependent on mechanical automation, but is incorporated in language and cognition. At this point, we might speak of hyper-real subsumption implying in it mental subsumption, the capture and re-formatting of the mind.

Neurology of Ants and the Evolution of Man

'The Net is an emblem of multiples. Out of it comes swarm being – distributed being – spreading the self over the entire web so that no part can say "I am the I" . . . It conveys the power both of Computer and Nature, which in turn convey a power before understanding.'[9]

In almost mystical terms, Kevin Kelly here outlines a philosophical vision of the replacement of conscious political control with the distribution of embedded rules of compliance inside the individual organism and within the superorganism.

> As very large webs penetrate the made world, we see the first glimpses of what emerges from that net – machines that become alive, and evolve, a neo-biological civilisation. There is a sense in which a global mind also emerges in a network culture. The global mind is the union of computer and nature, of telephones and human minds and more. It is a very large complexity of indeterminate shape governed by an invisible hand of its own. We humans will be unconscious of what the global mind ponders. This is not because we are not smart enough, but because the design of a mind does not allow the parts to understand the whole. The particular thoughts of the global mind – and its subsequent actions – will be out of our control and beyond our understanding.[10]

Kelly is well placed to see the current mutation as emergence of a neo-biological civilization: in a double process of becoming, the body is wired and automated by the insertion of electronic devices in the flow of communication, and the machine introduced to the network of biological complexity. The automaton and the cyborg are two different manifestations of the process. The automaton is a machine that behaves as an intelligent body, while the cyborg is a human body incorporating electronic devices.

In Kelly's vision, the creation of the net converges with the creation of a global interconnected mind that acts as an invisible hand leading individuals to merge with the swarm. 'The hive possesses much that none of its part possesses. One speck of a honeybee brain operates with a memory of six days; the hive as a whole operates with a memory of three months, twice as long as the average bee lives.'[11]

In the '70s, when the world capitalist strategy was veering towards deregulation and the dismantlement of the welfare state, the concept of socio-biology entered the ideological debate: the Darwinist concept of natural selection was transferred to the cultural and economic sphere, and biological self-regulation adopted as the paradigm of social evolution.

Edward Wilson was one of the prominent theorists of this kind of social Darwinism and developed his socio-biological concepts in books on the social history of insects, such as *The Superorganism*.

Nothing in the brain of the worker ant represents a blueprint of the social order. There is no overseer or brain caste who carries such a master plan in its head. Instead, colony life is the product of self-organisation. The superorganism exists in the separate programmed responses of the organisms that compose it. The assembly instructions the organisms follow are the developmental algorithms, which create the castes; together with the behavioural algorithms, which are responsible for moment-to-moment behaviour of the caste members. The algorithms of caste development and behaviour are the first level in the construction of a superorganism. The second level of construction is the genetic evolution of the algorithms themselves. Out of all possible algorithms, generating the astronomically numerous social patterns they might possibly produce, at least in theory, only an infinitesimal fraction have in fact evolved. The sets of algorithms actually realised, each of which is unique in some respect to a living species, are the winners in the arena of natural selection. They exist in the world as a select group that emerged in response to pressures imposed by the environment during the evolutionary history of the respective species.[12]

Speaking of leafcutter ants (several species of ants living in tropical parts of South, Central and North America) Wilson writes:

> Leafcutter colonies can be better understood as complex organic structures with a single purpose: the conversion of plant life into more colonies of leafcutter ants. They are civilisations designed by natural selection to replicate themselves in as many copies as possible before their inevitable death. Because they possess one of the most complex communication systems known in animals, as well as the most elaborate caste systems, air conditioned nest architecture, and populations in the millions, they deserve recognition as Earth's ultimate superorganisms . . . If visitors from another star system visited Earth a million years ago, before the rise of humanity, they might have concluded that leafcutter colonies were the most advanced societies this planet would ever be able to produce.[13]

The ants, bees, wasps and termites are among the most socially advanced non-human organisms of which we have knowledge. In biomass and impact on ecosystems, their colonies have been dominant elements of most of the land habitats for at least 50 million years. Social insect species existed for more than an equivalent span of time previously, but were relatively much less common. Some of the ants, in particular, were similar to those living today. It gives pleasure to think that they stung or sprayed formic acid on many a dinosaur that carelessly trampled their nests. The modern insect societies have a vast amount to teach us today. They show how it is possible to 'speak' in complex messages with pheromones. And they illustrate, through thousands of examples, how the division of labor can be crafted with flexible behavior programs to achieve an optimal

efficiency of a working group. Their networks of cooperating individuals have suggested new designs in computers and shed light on
how neurons of the brain might interact in the creation of the
mind.[14]

The ability to detect and interpret signs, the ability to
communicate and to fulfil tasks compatible with the needs of
the colony is an example of social life driven by automatisms
inscribed in the neurology of the ants.

How does a superorganism arise from the combined operation of tiny and short-lived minds?

The highly organised cooperative foraging of the leafcutters depends
on information transfer and social communication ... several
behavioural studies revealed a rich diversity of scent-guided behaviour and astounding odour sensitivity in leafcutter ants ... sensory
neurones carry the information about the odorant molecules to the
antennal lobes, which are part of the brain ... where sensory neurons
connect with projection neurons.[15]

Marx says (in the Introduction to *Grundrisse*) that the anatomy of man is the key to understanding the evolution of the
anatomy of the ape. At this point we might say that the
neurology of ants and bees is the key to understanding the
current evolution of man. The insertion of devices for cognitive automation, and the bio-genetical and psychopharma-
cological programming of the human brain are transforming
the anthroposphere into a swarm-like superorganism.

In the '70s a line of enquiry calling itself socio-biology
appeared on the philosophical scene. It presented itself as a
description of the overall logic of evolution, including the

natural evolution of man. As description, it was false and assumed natural selection as a given event in human affairs. Socio-biology itself, however, was rather a project, a political strategy, and in this sense, we should admit that it was successful.

Today, in fact, while political attention is captured by the fragmentary global civil war, in a separated sphere (of the bunker), the bio-info superorganism is emerging as the meeting point of bioengineering and cognitive automation. It is the implementation of a social engineering project that has led to natural selection being inscribed in the psycho-cultural composition of the social brain.

But this process of implementing the socio-biological vision is not without conflicts, without suffering, without laceration.

Late modernity has been described as the century of the self.[16] What's happening to self-perception in the current transition to the swarm?

The reshaping of the self is linked to the epidemics of psychotic behaviour and the booming economy of psychopharmacology accompanying the ongoing becoming of the swarm: this is going to be a central field of investigation for psychoanalytical and neurological reflection in our time.

The Exploding Self

Two articles on drugs appeared in the 19 April 2015 issue of the *New York Times*.

The first, 'Workers Seeking Productivity in a Pill Are Abusing ADHD Drugs' by Alan Schwarz, described the spread of Adderall among American professionals. Adderall contains a combination of amphetamine and dextroamphetamine, two central nervous system stimulants that affect brain and nerves, contributing to hyperactivity and impulse control.

In recent decades, millions of American children have been diagnosed with ADHD, with Ritalin as the suggested therapy. Now it is the turn of young cognitive workers, engaged in the market of attention: they take Adderall because they need to accelerate their mental performance in order to compete. Alan Schwartz interviewed some of them: 'Elisabeth, a Long Island native in her late twenties, said that not taking Adderall while competitors did would be like playing tennis with a wooden racket.'

On the same day in the same newspaper, an op-ed by Sam Quinones titled 'Serving All Your Heroin Needs', started with the notice that 'fatal heroin overdoses in America have almost tripled in three years', and goes on to describe the normalization of heroin distribution in American towns: a system that according to Quinones 'resembles pizza delivery'.

On 10 November 2015, the *New York Times* published the alarming article 'A.D.H.D. Rates Rise Around Globe, but Sympathy Often Lags' by Katherine Ellison about the spread of Attention Deficit Disorders worldwide.

> While global diagnoses of A.D.H.D. are on the rise, public understanding of the disorder has not kept pace. Debates about the validity of the diagnosis and the drugs used to treat it – the same that have long polarized Americans – are now playing out from Northern and Eastern Europe to the Middle East and South America.
>
> Data from various nations tell a story of rapid change. In

Germany, A.D.H.D. diagnosis rates rose 381 percent from 1989 to 2001. In the United Kingdom, prescriptions for A.D.H.D. medications rose by more than 50 percent in five years to 657,000 in 2012, up from 420,000 in 2007. Consumption of A.D.H.D. medications doubled in Israel from 2005 to 2012.

The surge in use of the medications has prompted scepticism that pharmaceutical firms, chasing profits in an $11 billion international market for A.D.H.D. drugs, are driving the global increase in diagnoses. In 2007, countries outside the United States accounted for only 17 percent of the world's use of Ritalin. By 2012, that number had grown to 34 percent.

I think diseases of this kind that affect the ability to focus on an object and the ability to produce a consistent flow of enunciation may be viewed as the signals of a process of psychological mutation that is marked by the externalization of the self. The fragmentation and acceleration of the flow of info-stimulation, the multitasking effect and the competitive pressure that is tied to the ability to follow the rhythm of the Infosphere are provoking the explosion of the centred self and a sort of psychotic deterritorialization of attention.

The intensification of the info-flow provokes a disturbance in the cognitive ability to detect and interpret signs, but simultaneously pushes us towards a swarm-like automation of the functioning of the mind. The self is both pressured from the outside world and replicated by the surrounding world of other minds. The faster the act of interpretation of info-stimulus, the more the process of interpretation is shared and homologated. The swarm mutation is proceeding both from the outside world and from the interaction with other minds.

5
Necro-Capitalism

Global Civil War?

The political theory of the past century resorted broadly to two models of interpretation in order to explain the evolution of the world. The first was the geopolitical model, based on the territorial players in the game: nation states, military alliances, geographical spaces defined by ethnicity, religion, nationality. The second was a socio-ideological model, based on the hypothesis that conflicts were motivated by economic interests and that the actors were social classes or political parties pursuing projects of social organization. It worked, as during the past century the historical process could be described as the interaction of the aforementioned models, and strategies of action could be conceived on that ground.

Even though according to Marx class struggle cannot be identified with a national project, the Russian Revolution linked and subordinated the destiny of the workers' movement in the world to the establishment of a new state, the Soviet Union. In the seventy years that followed the Revolution, class struggle has been indissolubly linked to the geopolitical. Western capitalism and Soviet socialism have turned into two military blocks in permanent conflict, and all social struggle has been subjected to the geopolitical destiny of the first socialist state – the authoritarian state whose force of attraction decreased until the point of its final collapse in 1989–91.

Because it subjected the social dynamics and autonomous movement of workers to the destiny of an imperial authoritarian state, the Leninist decision of 1917 and the ensuing militarization of class struggle can be understood as the beginning of the defeat of communism and of internationalism itself.

When, finally, the Soviet empire crumbled, its dismantlement resulted in the effective collapse of the communist project and of the workers' movement worldwide, paving the way for the neoliberal offensive.

The *nomenklatura* of communist establishment in Russia and in other territories of the former empire turned out to be themselves the perpetrators of the privatization of social services and of productive structures.

Class struggle has not been abandoned since the end of the Soviet empire, not at all: instead it has turned into a unilateral war against people's daily life, against salaries and social services, against the social civilization established over the last two centuries of modern progress. But over the recent decades, workers have been helplessly facing the neoliberal firing squad.

As an effect of the de-solidarization that followed the

worldwide defeat of socialism, the model of interpretation based on the concept of social conflict has surreptitiously been put aside, and the geopolitical model has seized the upper hand as the one to best describe the historical process.

The living subjectivities involved in such conflict have lost consciousness of their social dimension, and have redefined themselves in terms of national or religious belonging. Since the Yugoslav Wars, nation states have been re-motivated along ethnic and religious identities. This tendency has been exacerbated by the American wars and the subsequent rise of Islamist jihadism. At the end of 2015 (when I started writing this torturous book), the talk of world war was recurrent in public discourse and in the press.

Privatization of War

It would be inappropriate to name the current state 'world war' as with the conflicts of the past century.

The causes of the current looming war lie in the past two hundred years of the colonial impoverishment and humiliation of the majority of the world's population, in the philosophy of neoliberal competition and in the privatization of everything, including war itself.

War is being normalized: the stock markets no longer react to massacres. Instead, their main worry is the impending stagnation of the world economy. After every armed attack, by Islamists or by white supremacists, by improvised random murderers or by well-trained killers, the American people run to buy more weapons. The available supply of weapons is increasing not only in the arsenals of the national powers but also in the kitchens and bedrooms of normal families.

In December 2015, Michele Fiore, a Republican assembly-woman in Las Vegas posted a Merry Christmas greeting on Facebook. At first glance, it seems like any other holiday card: three generations in red shirts and jeans standing in front of a Christmas tree. But if you look again you see that Fiore, her adult daughters, their husbands, and one of her grandchildren are all holding firearms.

Privatization of war is an obvious feature of neoliberal deregulation, and the same paradigm has generated Halliburton and the Sinaloa Cartel, Blackwater and Daesh. The business of violence is one of the main branches of the global economy, and financial abstraction does not discriminate against criminal money.

The process of externalization and privatization is now provoking a worldwide civil war that is feeding on itself. According to Nicholas Kristof, 'In the last four years, more people have died in the United States from guns (including suicides and accidents) than Americans died in the wars in Korea, Vietnam, Afghanistan and Iraq combined.'[1]

We are not heading towards a third world war. There will be no declaration of war, but a proliferation of uncountable combat zones. There will be no unification of the fronts, but fragmented micro-conflicts and uncanny alliances with no general strategic vision.

'World war' is not the right term for this very original form of apocalypse we are now in. I call it 'fragmentary global civil war'.

The fragments are not converging, because the war is everywhere. According to Ash Carter, former American secretary of defense, 'Destructive power of greater and greater magnitude falls into the hands of smaller and smaller groups of human beings.'[2]

In conditions of war privatization, no geopolitical order of the world can be imagined, no consent among the conflicting religious tribes can be pursued. No beginning, no end because this war is endless, as it was decreed in 2001 by George Bush and Dick Cheney, who willingly fell into the trap set by bin Laden. From the Paradise where he certainly dwells, bin Laden looks upon the present emergence of the Caliphate of Death, smiling: so far, he can claim that the Army of Allah is winning the war.

Some American Republicans say that the spontaneous killing sprees that occur with regularity are the product of mental illness. They are right in a way, but they wrongly categorize what they label mental illness. This mental illness is not the rare malady of some isolated social dropout; it is the widespread consequence of panic, depression, precariousness and humiliation. These, too, are at the heart of the contemporary fragmentary global war, and they are spreading everywhere, rooted as they are in the legacy of colonialism and in the frantic competition of the everyday.

Neoliberal deregulation has given birth to a worldwide regime of necro-economy: moral prescriptions and legal regulations have been annulled by the all-encompassing law of competition. From its very beginning, Thatcher's philosophy prescribed war among individuals. Hobbes and Darwin and Hayek have been summoned to conceptualize the end of social civilization, the end of peace.

Forget about the religious or ideological labels of the agents of massive violence; look at their true natures. Take the Sinaloa Cartel and Daesh, then compare them to Blackwater and to Exxon Mobil. They have much more in common than not. Their shared goal is to extract a maximum of money from investment in the most exciting products of the contemporary economy: terror, horror and death.

Global Work Composition: Inside and Outside the Bunker

At the end of 2013, a group of Bay Area activists launched a protest campaign against the private buses that carried the everyday cognitive workers of the city to Google's Mountain View headquarters. These buses are bulky vehicles that the workers of the net corporation use as mobile offices. The nerds, in fact, are working all the time, with the merry awareness of being the protagonists of the ultimate virtualization of life and final step towards bunkerization. Leaving aside the immediate motivations of the protest (the protection of public space against the invasion of private transportation), this conflict sheds light on the new stratification of labour, and demands new conceptual tools. The composition of contemporary global society is structured around a fundamental separation between the inside-the-bunker social sphere and the outside-the-bunker social sphere.

The bunker is the area in which the financial class and the

cognitive workers live and work. This area can be outlined
in terms of technical environment or in terms of urban loca-
tion, and it is here where the main connective and recombinant functions are situated: the function of the financial decisions that dominate and exploit the whole cycle of production,
and the function of cognitive labour, mostly precarious but
protected to some extent, because it is strictly necessary to
the accumulation of capital.

Both of these functions are internally stratified and differ-
entiated, but the sphere in which all of its functionaries live
and produce is ever more wired, virtualized and sealed, separated from the territorial society that lives outside the bunker,
where industrial workers labour in factories and where the
growing areas of poverty and marginalization dwell.

The extra-bunker sphere is composed of all those people
who have no place inside the networked cycle. While they
can obviously own and use wired, technical devices for their
private lives and activities, their subsistence is based on a
direct relation to the physical matter of production. This is
the unprotected territory of the metropolis: industrial workers, the unemployed, migrants, refugees.

The old industrial bourgeoisie, too, were interested in
preserving the physical distinction of territory. Although
separated from the lower classes, the bourgeoisie lived in the
same urban space, and expected profits from the progress of
society as a whole and from the community's future
consumption.

Financial capital is not interested in the territory, nor in
the future of the community, as it has no contact with extra-
bunker spaces. Financial profit is realized in the dimension of
simultaneity and virtual exchange.

The financial class dwells in militarily protected gate communities, and takes holidays in simulated locations guarded by armies, where the snow is fake, the mountains are fake, the sea is fake and the human beings express fake sentiments. Furthermore, financial capital is not planning for any future, as the future is *now*, in the instantaneous valorization of virtual value and in the devastation of the radial spaces of physical territory.

Cognitive workers, indeed, are living in a halfway condition: as long as they are doing their job, they live inside the bunker, but as soon as they suspend their intercourse with the connected screen, as soon as they come out of the protected offices of their net corporation, they, too, sink into the metropolitan jungle.

Those who do not work directly in the networked or financial spheres are living outside of the bunker. Industrial workers have not decreased in their number, as the globalization of the labour market has introduced new masses of workers into the physical process of production, but they have lost any political or syndicated power. They are continuously threatened by the process of delocalization, and they have no possibility of intervening in decision-making processes, as they cannot access the bunker where the decisions are made and implemented.

The Ultimate Business

Outside the bunker (although subject to the bunker), the necro-economy is growing in extent and economic importance. Necro-work is the activity that produces profit for corporations whose actual product is death.

In his book *Gomorrah* – which is both a wonderful literary achievement and a detailed documentation of criminal activity in the area of Naples – Roberto Saviano has outlined the foundation of contemporary necro-economics.

> Profit, business, capital. Nothing else. One tends to think that the power determining certain dynamics is obscure, and so must issue from an obscure entity: the Chinese Mafia. A synthesis that cancels out all intermediate stages, financial transfers, and investments – everything that makes a criminal economic outfit powerful . . .
>
> You beat the competition on price. Same merchandise quality but at a 4, 6, 10 percent discount. Percentages no sales rep could offer, and percentages are what make or break a store, give birth to new shopping centres, bring in guaranteed earnings and, with them, secure bank loans. Prices have to be lower. Everything has to move quickly and secretly, be squeezed into buying and selling.[3]

The importance of criminal activity is growing and growing as an increasing number of young people at the urban peripheries of the world are left aside, humiliated and infuriated by competition and by the consumerist race.

Enterprises of terror and death are proliferating around the world: two outstanding examples are the Mexican narco-business and Daesh, the Syraqi Caliphate.

Joaquin Guzmán, better known as 'El Chapo' ('Shorty'), became Mexico's top drug kingpin in 2003 after the arrest of his rival Osiel Cárdenas of the Gulf Cartel. He is considered the 'most powerful drug trafficker in the world' by the United States Department of the Treasury. Every year from 2009 to 2011, *Forbes* ranked Guzmán as one of the most powerful people in the world, ranking him forty-first, sixtieth and fifty-fifth respectively. This made him the second most powerful man in Mexico, after Carlos Slim. He was named the tenth richest man in Mexico (and 1,140th in the world) in 2011, with a net worth of roughly US $1 billion. Not surprisingly, the magazine considered El Chapo as a deregulated entrepreneur who invests his capital in the ultimate business.

Dan Winslow has written extensively about the Mexican cartels and the Sinaloa Cartel in particular, which holds a preeminent importance in the history of the Narco-business.

The hellish Mexican situation was widely trumpeted in the international press at the end of 2014, when forty-three students of the Escuela Normal Rural de Ayotzinapa were kidnapped during an action of the police that, in this case (and in many, many others), was taken in coordination with local politicians linked to the narco-business.

According to the Italian journalist Federico Mastrogiovanni, the identification of the Mexican criminal industry as 'narco' is wrong, as the actual extension of criminal activities is not limited to drug-smuggling and production, but range from ransom to prostitution, from exploitation of slave labour to shale gas extraction. In his book *Ni vivos ni muertos* (Neither Alive Nor Dead), Mastrogiovanni focuses especially on the business of capturing and torturing human beings, and suggests that the narco-businesses are aiming to develop and expand into this market as well as others, such as a special interest in shale gas. In order to extract shale gas, it is necessary to dislodge the population of villages who live in areas like the Cuenca de Burgos. According to Mastrogiovanni, mass murders in the area have been planned and accomplished to achieve this purpose.

The Work of Terror

If the Mexican cartels are recruiting the young and unemployed from the poorest villages of the country (we might call them narco-proletarians), similarly the Caliphate recruits young men in the suburbs of London, Cairo, Tunis and Paris, then trains them to kidnap and slaughter people at random.

Thus an army of necro-workers is expanding around the world: the young unemployed who daily put their lives at risk in exchange for a salary, who develop a specialization in violence, torture and murder, and are paid for their criminal skills.

Daesh pays a monthly salary of US $450, while cashing funds from ransoms, oil revenues, and the fiscal imposition on millions of Sunni people. They deliver a postmodern Middle Age, but this is not backward at all, this is the anticipation of the future.

Dubiq, the advertising agency of the Islamic State has released a video in the style of any other advertisement: buy this product and you'll be happy.[4] Multiple camera angles, slick graphics, slow motion replays and even artificial wind give the whole thing a more dramatic feel.

Join the Allah Army and you'll find friends, warmth and well-being. Jihad is the best therapy for depression.

It is a message for feeble-minded people, for people who are suffering and crave warmth, strength of friendship, belonging. Not so different from the ads that we can see every day in the streets of our own cities, only more sincere on the subject of suicide. Suicide is crucial to this video: 6,500 soldiers in the US Army commit suicide every year, according to Dubiq. Americans die in anger, despair, while the soldiers of God die eager to meet the seventy virgins awaiting them in Paradise.

> The main reason why some young people are attracted to IS is because they are looking for jobs and it is easy to join it. IS has opened the door for Sunnis in the area that stretches from southern Baghdad to the outskirts of the city of Fallujah, by providing a good salary . . . things changed since the fall of Fallujah, as more young people joined IS. [Since then,] their duties have become daily and only about combat. [In return, they get] a monthly income of $400 to $500, but it is intermittent and not stable.[5]

It's easy to understand that Daesh will not be eradicated by the rhetorical speeches of François Hollande or by carpet bomb-ings. Their potential recruiting area, in fact, is large: millions of young Muslims who were ten years old when they watched the Abu Ghraib images on their TV screens and are now moneyless on the outskirts of London and Paris, of Cairo and Tunis, ready to join up and to slit Western throats in exchange for a salary. Why not? Business is business.

The emerging composition of work is changing in a frightening way: violence is no longer a marginal tool for social repression, but a normal mode of production, a special cycle of capital accumulation.

Is There a Way Out?

After the attacks in the centre of Paris on 13 November 2015, a nervous French president declared, 'The security pact takes precedence over stability pact. France is at war.'

Bin Laden's dream was in that moment fulfilled: a small group of fanatics provoked global civil war. Can it now be stopped?

Under the present conditions of long-lasting economic stagnation, in which the emerging markets are crumbling, the European Union is paralyzed and the promised economic recovery is elusive, it is hard to expect an awakening from this nightmare. The only imaginable way out of this hell is the end of financial capitalism, but this does not seem to be at hand.

Nevertheless, this is the only prospect we can pursue in this time of obscurantism: creating solidarity among the bodies of cognitive workers worldwide and building a techno-poetical platform for the collaboration of cognitive workers so as to liberate knowledge from religious dogma and from economic dogma, too.

Globalism has brought about the obliteration of modern universalism: capital flows freely everywhere and the labour market is globally unified, but this does not lead to the free circulation of women and men, nor to the affirmation of universal reason in the world. Rather, the opposite is happening: as the intellectual energies of society are captured by the network of financial abstraction, as cognitive labour is subjugated by the abstract law of valorization and human communication is transformed into abstract interaction among disembodied digital agents, the social body has become detached from the general intellect. The subsumption of the general intellect by the corporate kingdom of abstraction is depriving the living community of intelligence, understanding and affective emotion.

And the brainless body reacts. On one side, a huge wave of mental suffering, on the other side, the much-advertised cure for depression: fanaticism, fascism and war. And suicide at the end of it all.

Black Earth

Necro-labour is an essential part of the global economy, and terror a defining feature of power in the present neoliberal world. A second feature of contemporary power is a form of totalitarianism based on the perception of danger, fear and apocalypse.

In the book *Black Heart: The Holocaust as History and Warning*, Timothy Snyder argues that violent totalitarian drives can re-emerge as an effect of the contemporary observation of a looming apocalyptic danger. Such a sense is, indeed, actually spreading because of the environmental disruptions resulting from global warming.

> The planet is changing in ways that might make Hitlerian description of life, space and time more plausible. The expected increase of average global temperatures by four degrees Celsius this century would transform human life on much of the globe . . . Hitler was a child of the first globalisation, which arose under imperial auspices at the end of the nineteenth century. We are children of the second, that of the late twentieth century . . . When a global order collapses,

as was the experience of many Europeans in the second, third and fourth decades of the twentieth century, a simplistic diagnosis such as Hitler's can seem to clarify the global by referring to the ecological, supernatural, or the conspiratorial. When the normal rules seem to have been broken and expectations have been shattered, a suspicion can be burnished that someone (the Jews, for example) has somehow diverted nature from its proper course. A problem that is truly planetary in scale, such as climate change, obviously demands global solutions, and one apparent solution is to define a global enemy.

According to Snyder, when speaking of Nazism we should distinguish between history and warning: between the historical occurrence of the German outbreak of genocidal violence and the general implication that extreme totalitarianism and violence may emerge in situations of critical danger, in which a community can be easily united by the identification of an enemy. The effect of neoliberal globalization, the ensuing accelerated process of deterritorialization, and the aggressive competition unleashed can lead – and actually does lead – people to fiercely identify with a community of belonging, and to antagonize any ethnic or religious minority. The frightening trend that I detect in the present becoming of world history is the reaction of the declining white race against the deterritorialization that is sweeping over the economic, cultural and ethnic lines on the map of the world.

The emergence of Trump in American politics, and the proliferation of nationalist regimes in the Euro-Asian continent, may be read as the formation of an anti-globalist front that unifies Donald Trump and Vladimir Putin,

Jarosław Kacziński and Viktor Orbán, Marine Le Pen and Boris Johnson. This front is the expression of the pressure of the white working class defeated by financial globalism, and it is heading for a total opposition to the neoliberal elite.

6

Money Code and Automation

Neoliberal ideology has emphasized deregulation as the expression of a libertarian culture. Nothing is less true. Since the '80s, we have witnessed two simultaneous processes: the first is the abolition or weakening of legal limitations on the activity of enterprise, particularly of global corporations that have been displacing their investments from regulated areas to deregulated areas of the world. But the freedom of global enterprises has generally been the cause of the worsening condition of the lives and salaries of workers, and of the destruction of the natural and urban environment.

Furthermore, economic deregulation has not implied more freedom for citizens, particularly not for working citizens. The constraints have little by little shifted from the legal to the linguistic domain, especially in the techno-language of finance and crypto-contracts. Financial ethics are not a matter of law, moral rule or political injunction, rather they are inscribed in the technical rules that must be necessarily obeyed in order to gain access to the system.

The expanding pervasiveness of money in the economic sphere is the distinguishing feature of contemporary financial capitalism that can be named semio-capital, as signs take the prominent place in the process of production. Money is certainly a sign, and is one with a history. Whereas in industrial capitalism's past it was a referential sign, representing a certain quantity of physical things, today it is a self-referential sign that has acquired the power of both mobilizing and dismantling the social forces of production. Since the end of the regime of fixed monetary exchange, the arbitrary game of financial speculation has taken the central place in the global economy: the consequence is randomness in every relation between things and the precarization of every relation between persons. Simultaneously, however, finance has grown into the general force of inscription of an abstract automatic form of regulation in social life. The dynamics of debt, in particular, have penetrated and ultimately subjugated society, obliging people to interact with the banking system and to accept the language of investment.

At a certain point, particularly in the wake of the financial collapse of September 2008, many people who, like me, do not have any special interest in financial science have been obliged to try and understand the incomprehensible words of the financial agents, to try and resist the aggression that financial abstraction has waged against our concrete lives.

At the beginning of the new century, the so-called Dotcom Crash dissolved the illusion of an alliance between cognitive workers and venture capital that in the '90s enabled the creation and proliferation of the net. After the first crisis of the virtual economy in 2000, disempowered cognitive workers entered the cycle of precarization. Then the society at large was attacked by the menace of a metaphysical debt.

At the end of the '90s, Jean Baudrillard wrote the following:

> The debt will never be paid. No debt will ever be paid. The final counts will never take place. If time is counted, the missing money is beyond counting. The United States is already virtually unable to pay, but this will have no consequence whatsoever. There will be no judgment day for this virtual bankruptcy. It is simple enough to enter an exponential or virtual mode to become free of any responsibility, since there is no reference anymore, no referential world to serve as a measuring norm.[1]

Baudrillard's prediction has proven false: the orbitalization of the debt has failed. The debt which used to be in orbit has fallen down, and is haunting the economy. Facing the de-orbitalization of the debt, the financial class multiplied its attempts to create value from nothing. But to do that, the financial class is turning the products of social labour into nothing. As society pays the metaphysical debt, a sort of black hole has begun to swallow up the riches produced over the last two hundred years, particularly so in Europe. The credit derivatives market is the place where destruction replaces production. Since the '80s, when 'futures' became commonplace in deregulated markets, financial agencies started to invest their money paradoxically: if they win, they cash money; if they lose, they cash more money from the insurance on credit default swaps and other such financial tricks.

The old industrial model of accumulation was based on

the cycle M-G-M (Money-Goods-more Money). The new financial model of accumulation is based on the cycle M-P-M (Money-Predation-more Money), which implies the following: Money – social impoverishment – more Money. This is the origin of the black hole swiftly consuming the legacy of industrial labour and the very structures of modern civilization. As an attractor and destroyer of the future, financial capitalism captures energy and resources, transforming them into monetary abstraction: that is to say, into nothing. In 2008, a financial emergency was declared after the collapse of the American derivatives market and the failure of Lehmann Brothers. As a consequence, society at large was summoned to pay the reckless costs brought about by the financial dynamics.

Language and Money

The current financialization of the economy demands the self-referentiality of the monetary system as a condition. In fact, financial accumulation is essentially based on the automation of the relation between financial algorithms and the dynamics of production and exchange. The financial function (which once upon a time was dependent on the general interests of capitalism) has now become the automated language of the economy, a sur-codification subjecting the sphere of reality (production and exchange) to a mathematical rationale that is not inherent in the rationale of production itself.

Nixon's decision in 1971 to emancipate the American dollar from the universal regime of fixed exchange asserted the concept that the financial variable is independent from any referent, and is only based on the arbitrary power of self-regulation and self-asseveration. The creation of the digital web paved the way to the automation of the relation between financial code and economic dynamics, and social life was then subjected to financial semiotization.

Chomsky's structural theory is based on the idea that linguistic signs can be exchanged in the bank of shared structures: a common cognitive competence makes the exchange possible. Language is therefore, like money, a general equivalent, universal translator of different goods. We can exchange everything with money, as we can exchange everything with words.[2]

But money (like language, of course) is also a tool for the mobilization of energies, a pragmatic act of self-expansion. In the sphere of financial capitalism, money is less an indicator than a factor of mobilization. It is suitable to provoke participation or submission. Look at the reality of debt, look at the awful effects of impoverishment and exploitation that debt provokes in the body of society. Debt is a transformation of money into blackmail. Money, which was supposed to be the measure of value, has been turned into a tool for psychic and social subjugation. The metaphysical debt links money, language and guilt. Debt is guilt, and as guilt it is entering the domain of the unconscious, to shape language according to structures of power and submission.

Language and money have something in common: they are nothing in the physical world, but still they move everything in human history. Words move people to believe, words forge expectations and the impulse to act in the pursuit of goals. Words are tools for persuasion and for the mobilization of psychic energies. Money acts similarly, based on trust and the belief that a piece of paper represents everything that can be bought and sold in the world.

In 'Money: The Poor Man's Credit Card', Chapter 14 of *Understanding Media*, McLuhan writes:

> Money talks, because money is a metaphor, a transfer, and a bridge. Like words and language, money is a storehouse of communally achieved work, skill, and experience. Money, however, is also a specialist technology like writing; and as writing intensifies the visual aspect of speech and order, and as the clock visually separates time from space, so money separates work from the other social functions. Even today money is a language for translating the work of the farmer into the work of the barber, doctor, engineer, or plumber. As a vast social metaphor, bridge, or translator, money – like writing – speeds up exchange and tightens the bonds of interdependence in any community.[3]

Money is a tool for the simplification of social relations, and makes possible the automation of acts of enunciation. While the industrial automaton was mechanical, thermodynamic and consisted 'of numerous mechanical and intellectual organs so that workers themselves are cast merely as its conscious linkages', the digital automaton is electro-computational, involves the nervous system and unfolds in networks of electronic and nervous connection.[4] The bio-informational automaton is the product of the insertion of the digital automaton in the flow of socio-linguistic interactions.

Abstraction and Automation

During the last century, abstraction has been the main tendency of the general history of the world in the field of art, language and economics. Abstraction can be defined as the mental extraction of a concept from a series of real experiences, but it can be also defined as the separation of conceptual dynamics from bodily processes. Since the time Marx spoke of 'abstract labour' to refer to the working activity as separate from the useful production of concrete things, we know that abstraction is a powerful engine. Thanks to abstraction, capitalism has detached the process of valorization from the material process of production. As productive labour turns into a process of info-production, abstraction becomes the main source of accumulation, and the condition of automation. Automation is the insertion of abstraction into the machinery of social life, and consequently it is the replacement of an action (physical and cognitive) with a technical engine. Taking the view of cultural history, the first part of the twentieth century is marked by the emancipation of signs from a strictly referential function: this may be seen as the general trend of late modernity, the prevailing tendency in literature and art as in science and politics.

In the second part of the century, the monetary sign, however, reclaims its autonomy, and since Nixon's decision, after a process of monetary deregulation, the arbitrary self-definition of monetary dynamics has been firmly established: money shifts from referential to self-referential signification. This is the condition for the automation of the monetary sphere, and for the submission of social life to this sphere of abstraction.

Automation, which is electronic, does not represent physical work so much as programmed knowledge. As work is replaced by the sheer movement of information, money as a store of work merges with informational forms of credit.[5]

Retracing the history of money, from exchange commodity to representative money to standard value to electronic abstraction, McLuhan writes:

> The Gutenberg technology created a vast new republic of letters, and stirred great confusion about the boundaries between the realms of literature and life. Representative money, based on print technology, created new speedy dimensions of credit that were quite inconsistent with the inert mass of bullion and of commodity money. Yet all efforts were bent to make the speedy new money behave like the slow bullion coach. J. M. Keynes stated this policy in *A Treatise on Money*: Thus the long age of Commodity Money has at last passed finally away before the age of Representative Money. Gold has ceased to be a coin, a hoard, a tangible claim to wealth, of which the value cannot slip away so long as the hand of the individual clutches the material stuff. It has become a much more abstract thing – just a standard of value; and it only keeps this nominal status by being handed round from time to time in quite small quantities amongst a group of Central Banks.[6]

Only when it is abstracted (that is, separated from the referent, and disembodied) can monetary dynamics be automated, submitted to the rules of a non-referential sphere of signification and the attribution of value. Information takes the place of things, and finance – which once used to be the sphere where productive projects could meet capital, and where capital could meet productive projects – emancipates itself from the constraints of physical production: the process of capital valorization (increase of money invested) no longer passes through the creation of use value. As the referent is cancelled and financial accumulation is enabled by the mere circulation of money, the production of goods becomes superfluous to financial expansion. The accumulation of abstract value depends on the subjugation of the population to debt, and on the predation of existing resources. This emancipation of capital accumulation from the production of useful things results in a process of annihilation of social welfare.

In the sphere of financial economy, the acceleration of circulation and valorization implies the elimination of the concrete usefulness of products because the faster information circulates, the faster value is accumulated. Purely financial information is the fastest of things, while the production and distribution of goods is slow. The process of the realization of capital, namely the exchange of goods with money, slows the pace of monetary accumulation. The same happens in the field of communication: the less meaning the message has the faster it moves, given that production and interpretation of meaning take time, while the circulation of pure information without meaning is instantaneous.

In the last twenty years, computers, electronic exchanges, dark pools, flash orders, multiple exchanges, alternative trading venues, direct access brokers, OTC derivatives and high-frequency traders have totally changed the financial landscape and particularly the relation between human operators and self-directing algorithmic automatons. The more you remove the reference to physical things, to physical resources and the body, the more you can accelerate the circulation of financial flows. This is why, at the end of this process of abstraction-acceleration, value does not emerge from a physical relationship between work and things, but rather from the infinite self-replication of virtual exchanges of nothing with nothing.

Inscription of Rules

Some open-minded techno-financial agents, as well as groups of social activists, are promoting the idea that alternative currencies can be useful tools for undoing the financial trap from the inside.

The open-minded financial agents are inspired by the libertarian persuasion that the economic sphere has to be free from the state and from centralized monetary control. They are looking for a possibility for the democratization of the financial sphere.

I don't know if the function of money can be subverted or if money can be used as a tool for disentangling social life and production from financial capitalism that presently uses monetary dynamics as a tool for subjugating knowledge and work.

Experience says that money can act as an automator, *the* ultimate automator of social life. Experience shows that removing spaces in which we live from monetary exchange and codification (insolvency, non-monetary exchange) is the way to create spaces for autonomy.

Insolvency is the most effective way to resist the financial blackmail that is systematically destroying society. But organized insolvency is only possible when social solidarity is strong, and in the present condition the links of solidarity are weak.

Although there have been mass protests in the streets, people have not lately been able to keep solidarity alive for long. This is why insolvency – the active refusal to pay debt and undeserved taxation, the refusal to pay for basic services, the permanent occupation of spaces and buildings, and the sabotage of austerity – has not really grown roots in the social scene over these last years.

Rudimentary forms of alternative currencies for local exchange have appeared lately in many places across Europe, adding to experiences like the sharing of time and basic services and goods. But community currencies can only become a significant form of exchange when social solidarity is strong enough to nurture trust and mutual help.

More sophisticated forms of alternative currencies have been promoted by highly skilled programmers: Bitcoin is the best known of these. Generating money is a technical problem, but replacing financial money with alternative money is a problem of trust.

Alternative currencies could serve as a game changer, this is quite possible, and up to a certain point it is already happening. But it is not clear how these alternatives can act as surrogates for a more fundamental lack of social solidarity.

Algorithmic money, however, can act as the ultimate tool for automation: automation of behaviour, of language, of relation, automation of evaluation and exchange. Regardless of the intentions of Bitcoin miners, their monetary action is going to heighten the level of automation in the sphere of social exchange.

What is interesting to me is the techno-linguistic automation of the relations among people: economic and financial relations are no longer the object of an ethical negotiation or of a political decision. They are more and more inscribed in the code that gives access to a certain service, or to a certain possibility of having a job, and so on and so forth.

Coding personal relationships into programming language is the current tendency: crypto-money and crypto-contracts transform ever more the relations among people into the execution of programming, into a sequence of acts that one must accomplish in order to access the following step. The normative function of law is replaced by the automatic implication of human agents reduced to merely operational functions. The overcoming of the industrial system has been enabled by the translation of physical acts into information. The automation of linguistic interaction and the replacement of cognitive and affective acts with algorithm sequences and protocols is the main trend of the current mutation.

III
Possibility

In the third part of this book, I speak of possibility. My basic assumption is this: notwithstanding the darkness of the present, notwithstanding looming war and widespread resentment, notwithstanding the impotence of political will, a possibility lies in the structural constitution of the present world. It is a possibility of emancipation, enrichment and peace. This possibility is stored in the cooperation among the knowledge workers of the world. The content of this possibility is the liberation of human time from the constraints of labour and the full replacement of human labour time with technology. This liberation would not merely bring about an improvement in social relations, a redistribution of salary and of resources, and the end of massive unemployment.

It would also create the possibility for the displacement of social energies from the field of economies and the production of (often useless and damaging) goods to the field of care, self-care and education. The current social pathology is largely to be seen as an effect resulting from exploitation, economic competition, and the precariousness of salaries. Replacing human labour time with machines is not only a possibility at hand, but an urgent necessity for relieving environmental devastation, and for reducing the nervous stress that is choking social life and world peace.

The possibility lies in the social brain, in the social organization of knowledge and culture. As long as we are able to imagine and to invent, as long we are capable of thought independent from power, we will not be defeated. The problem is that the forces of darkness are trying to subdue thought, imagination and knowledge under the rule of greed and the rule of war.

If they do succeed in submitting knowledge to the logic of profit and violence, they will destroy everything. If they do not succeed in their intent, no matter how much destruction the forces of darkness can bring about, the cognitive workers of the world will find the energy and the creativity to resurrect the old dream of egalitarianism, social autonomy and happiness.

7

Conundrum

The virtual is not just the potential latent in matter, it is the potential of
potential. To hack is to produce or apply the abstract to information and
express the possibility of new worlds, beyond necessity.

McKenzie Wark, *Hacker Manifesto*

Capitalism is dead, and we are living inside its corpse, franti-
cally looking for a way out of the rotting putridity, and not
finding it.

Until now.

The cycle of profit accumulation and growth was based
on the extraction of surplus value from salaried labour and
from the production of use value translated into exchange
and valorization. That cycle is exhausted: use value is
produced, but the useful no longer produces surplus.

GDP growth is no longer an especially useful way of measuring the
health of modern economies. Many of the most important developments in the modern economy contribute little to official GDP

figures. Browsing on Wikipedia, watching videos on YouTube, and searching for information on Google add value to people's lives, but because these are digital goods that have zero price, official GDP figures will consistently downplay their impact. Improvements in efficiency, which reduce costs, have negative impact on GDP. Consider solar panels: their installation boosts GDP initially, but thereafter the savings in oil or gas reduce GDP.[1]

Capitalism is the shell that contains both activity and invention, but transforms everything that is useful into monetary value, and every concrete act of production into abstraction. Capitalism is a semiotic code that translates concrete activity into abstract value, and the translation implies that the concrete world of experience is depleted.

Automation

Since the days when I was a young militant in the Italian political organization *Potere operaio*, around 1968, I have been persuaded that technological innovation was destined to replace human labour, and that the main goal of the workers' movement was to fight for the reduction of working hours.

Salaried work implies the subjection of activity to the profit-oriented economy, and the history of social struggles can be read as a search for autonomy from the entangling relation of salaried work.

In fact, the long wave of struggles and social mobilizations that shook the Western world and particularly my country before and after '68 could be summarized in a few words: workers want to work less and earn more.

To increase productivity and also to control sabotage and rebellion, capitalists are investing in technology and introducing machines to automate of the production process.

Automatic machines can do repetitive work. They can also take 'decisions', though only in the light of circumstances previously foreseen by human beings. We propose to discuss the limitations of automatic machines within their own field of performing repetitive tasks and of taking certain sorts of 'decisions'. The development of automation is limited by the technical knowledge of engineers, the cost of constructing automatic machines, the demand for automatic machinery, and the availability of trained specialists capable of designing, constructing and operating such machines. From a purely technical point of view there is no doubt that automatic machines can be devised to perform any repetitive task more rapidly, more accurately and with greater care than human workers.[2]

At the end of the '60s, I convinced myself that the technological advancements of electronics and robotics, were paving the way for the liberation of social life from the obligation of work.

Fifty years later, it is crystal clear that my prediction was wrong.

Now, in the second decade of the twenty-first century, I must acknowledge that people are working much more, and cashing much less, than they did three decades ago: in fact, the political force of the workers' movement has largely vanished.

My prediction was wrong because I did not take into account the cultural resistance against the prospect of liberation from work, the imbalances in the economic development of the different areas of the world, the effects of global competition in a profit-oriented economy, and, last but not least, the contradictory role played by the movement of industrial workers, particularly by the communist parties and by the unions in large parts of the world.

Nevertheless, I do not disclaim my early theoretical move. Though my prediction has been resoundingly proved wrong, the problem still exists more than ever.

Work, science and technology have cooperated to a point of widening automation that has enormously increased the productivity of work, paving the way for a massive reduction in necessary work time. But this has still not led to a reduction of the hours that people devote to salaried work in their lives. On the contrary, both industrial and cognitive workers are working today much more than in the '60s and '70s. While the figures concerning unemployment and precarity are increasing, the globalization of the labour market has destroyed the old regulations and limitations on work time.

In the past decades, thinkers like Rifkin and Gorz have predicted the end of work as a linear consequence of technological development, but reality has contradicted their prediction and things have gone in a very different direction. Not improvement, but a worsening of the workers' conditions, not liberation but the return of forms of precarious enslavement, not empowerment, but a widespread sense of powerlessness – this is the present reality of work when compared to the sociological imagination of the second half of the twentieth century.

In the book *Post-Work*, published in 1998, the editors Stanley Aronowitz and Jonathan Cutler retraced the general lines of the history of work time in America. The struggle for shorter hours was one of the most important items on the agenda of the workers' movement. A steady decline in the hours of work throughout the nineteenth and the twentieth centuries has been the chief achievement of the progressive action of unions.

Then something happened in the last part of the past century, in paradoxical simultaneity with the implementation of digital technology that enormously accelerated productivity and created a new dimension of semiotic work.

The globalization of capital, the creation of transnational corporations, and the erosion of national borders has led to the utter deterritorialization of the labour market, placing labour in competition with itself at a global scale, while the unions and the progressive political parties (communists included) remained largely imprisoned within national borders and did not see the danger of globalization or the deregulation of the labour market. Subsequently, the most important achievement of the labour movement – the decrease in hours worked, and the consequent liberation of social energies for self-care, education and pleasure – has been reversed.

'The Post-Work Manifesto', in Cutler and Aronowitz's book, states, 'Standards of living are not increasing, quality leisure time is not being enjoyed, stress and its social manifestations are rampant, and the golden future we were all planning is collapsing fast.'[3] More work hours provoke more stress, less self-care, less time for children and less time for education. Furthermore, it is obvious that more work hours bring about general unemployment: while a part of the working population is forced to prolong their work hours, a growing number of people are pushed into a condition of unemployment, forced to accept any kind of precarious job.

After years of social crisis and rising unemployment rates in the United States, Obama's policy of quantitative easing has reversed the unemployment trend and a surge in employment has been widely hailed by economists.

But is this really an improvement for social life? The answer comes from Frank Bruni, in a column for the *New York Times*, 'The new jobs don't feel as sturdy as the old ones. It takes more hours to make the same money or support the same lifestyle. Students amass debt. Upward mobility increasingly seems a mirage, a myth.'[4]

The general trend of the epoch is well expressed in this sentence, 'It takes more hours to make the same money or support the same lifestyle.'

This signals a regression for humanity as a whole.

The Conundrum

The relation between work, technology and automation under the conditions of a capitalist economy can be described as a conundrum.

In plain terms, we can describe this conceptual labyrinth in the following way: the application of intellectual abilities on the work process causes an increase of productivity, and therefore makes possible a reduction of the work time necessary for the production of goods needed for social survival.

Even if the population grows (as it did over the last forty years or so), even if the physical and cultural necessities of the world population expand (as they did over the last decades, thanks to the extension of the market throughout the world and the access to industrial consumption by masses of people), the productivity increase enabled by the automation of industrial tasks is largely sufficient for a reduction of the labour time of each individual.

Nevertheless, the plain terms of this description do not coincide with the dynamics of capitalist economy. The contents of the process of production (manual work, scientific knowledge, technical skills, automation of industrial tasks, automation of cognitive tasks) have to be appreciated in relation to the container: the capitalist economy, whose features are shaping and modelling the application of the abstract technical possibilities.

My focus here is on the relation between the content and the container.

Beware: the container is not merely a container. It is a semiotizer, a formal paradigm, that has been shaped by economic interests, cultural norms and expectations, political institutions, military structures and so on. As a semiotizer, the container fabricates semiotic models for the organization of the contents (daily life, language, knowledge, technology).

Social imagination is shaped by the container, so the contents of social activity are modelled according to the paradigm of accumulation and growth, while the contents (knowledge, labour, creativity) produce possibilities that exceed the container.

The relation between the semiotizer and the living contents is a conundrum, and should be investigated as an enigma, not as a secret.

A secret is, in fact, the hidden truth of a quandary. With a secret, you know that a true answer exists, although it is hidden and protected. Find the key to the box and you'll find the true answer inside.

By contrast, an enigma is inscrutable: there is no central hidden truth to discover, no definitive answer to the question. An enigma is an infinite quandary that can be only decided on by an act of ethico-aesthetic intuition, not by a mathematical solution as with a problem.

Speaking of the anthropological meaning of infinite regress, Paolo Virno writes that there is a moment when you feel that you have been searching enough, and then you decide.[5]

The enigmatic feature of ethical questioning and judgement resides in the following: there is no truth, there is no solution to the problem and, strictly speaking, there is no problem. Only the vibrational condition of wandering in a space of possibility.

In the social field the decider is force. The capitalist semiotizer has force, while the forms of life that feel contained and squeezed, crammed and compressed inside that formal container do not have enough force to crack the container and break out.

Refusal of Work in Precarious Times

The expression 'refusal of work' has had a wide circulation in Italian workerist literature since the end of the '60s, reflecting a particular anthropological situation: the massive migration of young people from the southern areas of the country to the northern industrial cities. Those people resented the change in their lives. Coming from the lazy sunny days of their Mediterranean childhood and jumping into the fog and the noise of the dark space of the factories, they felt uneasy, and restless. When they entered into contact with the metropolitan culture of the students, their distaste for work turned into a cultural protest against alienation.

Their question was: is this life?

No, this meaningless repetition of meaningless gestures was (and is) not life.

Refusal of work was a declaration of war against boredom and sadness, based on the special condition of a generation of workers growing up in a decade of mass education, when cultural attitudes and existential expectations were exploding.

Nevertheless, it would be wrong to restrain the concept of refusal of work to that historical situation, because it has a wider meaning: resistance to work is the source of technical innovation inasmuch as it enables the reduction of labour time.

In the peculiar constellation of the second part of the past century, social consciousness and techno-evolution coincided, and the potencies of knowledge opened the door to the emancipation of life from salaried work, so that the digital network could be hailed as the ultimate force of liberation. But emancipation from work is not a purely technical process. It presupposes political awareness and a deep transformation of cultural expectations. Both have been missed. The unions have opposed the introduction of labour-saving technologies and have instead dedicated their energies and influence to the defence of jobs and of existing working conditions. They linked their identity to the industrial composition of labour, and have turned into a conservative force that opposes innovation, allowing only financial capitalists to exploit the techno opportunity.

Social consciousness and techno-evolution diverged at that point, and at that moment we entered the age of techno-barbarianism: innovation provoked precarity, richness created mass misery, solidarity became competition, the connected brain was uncoupled from the social body and the potency of knowledge was uncoupled from social welfare.

Nevertheless, the general intellect's potency is still active and well. It is unable to trigger a process of social emancipation, however, because the conjunction among bodies has grown precarious and fragile, while the connection among disembodied brains has grown permanent, all encompassing and obsessional, to the point of replacing life with the spectral projection of life on the ubiquitous screen.

During the last decades, innovation in technology has enormously enhanced work productivity and created the situation for a potential abundance of goods.

Is this the proof of a superior efficiency of capitalism? Not at all, it is the achievement of the cooperation of millions of cognitive workers worldwide. It is the effect of creativity and knowledge: it is engineers, designers, philosophers who have made this possible. They have enriched and improved daily life, if we look at it in consideration of use value.

If we translate innovation into the language of the economy, if we replace 'use value' with the logic of valorization and capital accumulation, everything takes on a different shape.

Notwithstanding the incredible expansion of the universe of useful goods and services, the distribution of wealth is so unequal and unbalanced that richness seems to be regressing and life seems to be getting worse and worse.

In economic terms, in fact, growth means increase of the gross national product in terms of value, of monetary wealth. The capitalist code transforms the expansion of the useful into financial accumulation and the impoverishment of daily life. The prescription of growth as a cultural model acts on social production as a semiotic tangle that provokes a distortion and transforms possible richness into actual misery.

In 2015, oil production in the world had grown so abundant that the price per barrel fell to an unprecedented low. The same can be said of steel production. In the same period, demand fell in every country of the world. This conjuncture was described as a catastrophe by economists who expected an overall collapse of the economy worldwide: over-production, deflation, unemployment. But this was proof that capitalism implies a transliteration of the real world of usefulness into the abstract world of value, recoding richness into misery, abundance into scarcity, potency into powerlessness.

Fake Companies

At 9:30 a.m. on a sunny weekday, the phones at Candelia, a purveyor of sleek office furniture in Lille, France, rang steadily with orders from customers across the country and from Switzerland and Germany. A photocopier clacked rhythmically while more than a dozen workers processed sales, dealt with suppliers and arranged for desks and chairs to be shipped.

Sabine de Buyzer, working in the accounting department, leaned into her computer and scanned a row of numbers. Candelia was doing well. Its revenue that week was outpacing expenses, even counting taxes and salaries. 'We have to be profitable,' Ms. de Buyzer said. 'Everyone's working all out to make sure we succeed.'

This was a sentiment any boss would like to hear, but in this case the entire business is fake. So are Candelia's customers and suppliers, from the companies ordering the furniture to the trucking operators that make deliveries. Even the bank where Candelia gets its loans is not real.

More than 100 Potemkin companies like Candelia are operating today in France, and there are thousands more across Europe. In Seine-St.-Denis, outside Paris, a pet business called Animal Kingdom sells products like dog food and frogs. ArtLim, a company in Limoges, peddles fine porcelain. Prestige Cosmetique in Orleans deals in perfumes. All these companies' wares are imaginary.

France has over 100 staged companies where jobless workers get training, like the pet boutique Animal Kingdom. These companies are all part of an elaborate training network that effectively operates as a parallel economic universe. For years, the aim was to train students and unemployed workers looking to make a transition to different industries. Now they are being used to combat the alarming rise in long-term unemployment, one of the most pressing problems to emerge from Europe's long economic crisis.

Ms. de Buyzer did not care that Candelia was a phantom operation. She lost her job as a secretary two years ago, and has been unable to find steady work. Since January, though, she had woken up early every weekday, put on makeup and gotten ready to go the office. By 9 a.m. she arrives at the small office in a low-income neighbourhood of Lille, where joblessness is among the highest in the country.

While she doesn't earn a paycheque, Ms. de Buyzer, 41, welcomes the regular routine. She hopes Candelia will lead to a real job, after countless searches and interviews that have gone nowhere.[6]

This incredible story reads like a novel by Philip K. Dick. It's about a world in which people get up early in the morning and go to work in a place that produces nothing and pays no salary. But it is not a novel, it is the description of a society blinded by its own preconceptions, mainly the dogma of salaried work and economic growth.

People have been educated to believe that work is the grounds of identity and dignity, they have socialized only in the context of their work environment, so they grow depressed to realize that their work is no longer necessary.

Depression is a consequence of the obsessional conflation of identity and work, and of the internalization of the link between survival and the divestiture of one's own life. This link we call a salary. But the usefulness of our skills and knowledge cannot be reduced to abstract exchangeability. The useful activity of millions of cognitive workers is actually materialized in the universal machine that replaces human work.

Even if this machine is denied, hidden, forgotten, it produces effects in the social unconscious. And the social unconscious feels the absurdity of the machinery that forces us to give up life in order to survive.

8

Superstition

Common Sense

In an article published by the *Guardian* in February 2016, 'Global Markets Are No Longer Obeying Economic Common Sense', Mark Blyth notes, 'One of the oddest things about 2016, so far at least, is how economic common sense is being twisted in all sorts of ways to explain what's going on in the global economy.'

What is common sense? What, in particular, does common sense mean in the domain of the economy? Common sense is the product of experience, but today common sense is out of order because the processes that economists are studying (production, exchange, technology, labour . . .) have changed so deeply that they can no longer be grasped with the conceptual tools that were developed out of our experience of the past.

Those concepts are like old eyeglasses that distort the surrounding reality and persuade society to perform acts that produce paradoxical effects.

Think of the so-called 'quantitative easing'.

What's the use of pouring huge amounts of money into the banking system? What's the use of pushing enterprises to invest money, when demand is going down as an effect of labour market globalization? 'Globalization, and concerted action for thirty years by the political right, has killed the ability of labour to demand higher wages, hence record inequality and super low inflation.'[1]

What's the use of obliging people to work more and more when the products of their work are not needed, not demanded and, most important, could be produced by machines?

The basic concepts of economic knowledge are misleading: 'Now we find ourselves in a post-crisis world in which the old tricks no longer work despite growth at 1.5 percent, inflation at 0.5 percent and interest rates in some places at minus 0.25 percent.'[2]

The contemporary economy is based on the semiotic coding of our relation to resources, production, technology and life. Social imagination is shaped by the impending blackmail of superstition.

An act of transliteration (recoding) is inscribed in the economy, and this recoding is not only a linguistic act: it is the source of financial predation, of the devastation of enormous amounts of goods and resources, and of the increasing inequality in the distribution of wealth.

The nomination of social relations is part of the process of internalization of capitalism as a natural form. We designate certain kinds of human activity 'work': time exchanged for a salary, the source of the accumulation of capital.

Activity may be joyful and enriching, but as it is transliterated into work it is devoiced of meaning and transformed into repetition. In order to become salaried work, activity must submit to the rules of repetition – no matter how creative the activity might be in itself.

Technology enables the enhancement of social experience, and particularly makes it possible to work less and enjoy more. But as soon as it is transliterated into economic terms, technology fuels frantic hyperactivity and competition on the one hand and unemployment on the other.

The economic language is based on the translation of the capitalist code into a social gestalt, a perceptual scheme acting as the generator of pre-formatted forms. The economic nomination of useful reality acts as a transformer of perception, and turns profit, growth and accumulation into the code of the emanation of things.

Work, salary, accumulation and exchange-value are not natural givens but socio-semiotic conventions. Conventions, however, are not only signs marking real life ex post, they are also frames of signification that are pre-forming and formatting our expectations and our modes of interaction.

Work is the keyword of the semio-economic gestalt. We are lured to identify our living activity with work, and we are forced to rely on salaried work for survival.

Competition is the mantra of the hegemonic neoliberal religion: compete in order to work more; work more in order to compete. Lower the salary in order to compete, and compete in order to be paid (less).

Why work more? The world is already saturated with objects, and yet we cannot stop producing more useless and obnoxious things because of economic superstition. Furthermore, the goods that we do need could be produced with less and less work.

Translating the potency of knowledge and of technology into the language of capitalist economy implies the subjugation of millions of cognitive workers to the rationale of the past: private profit and growth.

The reality of abundance is translated into the semiotic grid of scarcity.

> The ritual of overwork today is a totally constructed fact rather than anything bound by physical necessity. Moreover, as a social meme, it has colonized almost every other sphere of life ... The for-profit firm is an outmoded social institution that has outlived its utility for most of those involved. Society has left it behind, which is why it is clinging on to us so forcefully. Capitalism and its fetishisation of private property are swimming against the tide.[3]

In the old industrial world, when the process of production was essentially based on the mechanical transformation of matter, value could be easily defined in terms of time necessary for the manufacture of a product. Now the definition of value has become random and volatile because mental work is hard to translate into uniformed temporal standards: in the field of semiotic production, the old rules of valorization are dissolving, and the attribution of value lies on simulation, cheating and sheer violence.

Inconsonance

The dynamic of innovation has grown inconsonant with the semiotic code of capitalism that interprets and organises production technology and knowledge according to the rationale of accumulation and growth.

However, the breakdown of historical communism and the dismantlement of social solidarity have made any alternative to capitalism unthinkable.

The expectation of infinite expansion, deeply entrenched in the late modern psyche, is a trap. Only new expectations based on the recoding of the technological environment may enable the social organism to adapt to a condition of long-lasting un-growth. Redistribution of wealth, equality, sobriety, solidarity and friendship – these are the keywords of the possible and needed cultural transformation. But it seems that the majority of governments in the world are unable to see this possibility and necessity, as they are blinded by the overwhelming force of the economic superstition: work and salary, salaried work.

Superstition: an unfounded belief, a deception that deforms perception of real events and provokes inconsequential actions. In the past industrial age, the category of salary was able to signify human activity under conditions of scarcity, though often these were artificially engendered as in the case of the early modern English enclosure. But today the scarcity regime is over, as technological evolution in the last decades (and predictably in the next decades) enables the unprecedented increase of productivity that has resulted in the abundance that should be differently distributed.

Digital mutation and global finance have torpedoed the rules presiding over the old industrial system: the relation between value and labour time or between monetary dynamics and the productive function of the enterprise crumbles. Precarity undermines every form of collaboration. We have entered what Baudrillard envisioned as the random sphere of floating values. In this sphere, value can

no longer be based on labour time. While the global economy stagnates, a new push towards automation comes from
researchers and developers. The intersection of artificial
intelligence and the net opens the door to a new generation
of automatons; this new generation will not only replace
mechanical labour based on repetition, but also cognitive
labour based on selection and difference. As Paul Mason
warns, the 'coming wave of automation will hugely dimin-
ish the amount of work needed, not just to subsist but to
present a decent life for all.'[4]

This trend is fuelling anxiety and provoking hostile political reactions. The fear of automation has come and gone in
waves, as Richard Freeman points out:

> Not so long ago, economists and others downplayed talk of the
> robotization of work. The Depression Era fear among technocrats
> that machines would create permanent joblessness had proved false.
> The great automation scare of the 1960s never panned out. Most
> economists believed humans would never lose their advantage over
> machines in tasks requiring judgment and dexterity in uncertain,
> changing environments.[5]

Today such complacency is washed away. High-tech companies are investing massively in research for the replacement
of workers with intelligent automatons.

Larry Page has speculated that the next steps in labour-
replacing technology are hardly compatible with the forty-
hour work week. Nevertheless, people do spend eight or
nine hours per day performing low-paid tasks and are obliged
to work until the age of sixty-seven and more, while the
unemployment rate is rising.

In the years of social autonomy during the 1960s and 1970s, in many places in the world and particularly in Europe, the capitalist trend was provisionally suspended and also reversed: amid struggles, strikes and negotiations, industrial workers managed to get a reduction of the weekly work time to forty hours maximum.

Social solidarity and worker insubordination impelled engineers to develop time-saving technologies, so reducing overall work time. That was an ambivalent move: it paved the way to better living conditions, but it was also a threat against the existing composition of labour. The unions perceived technology as a danger, and opposed the implementation of such labour-saving devices, proving themselves unable to deal with technological change.

In this dynamic lies the source of the neoliberal triumph, and the emergence of a monstrous paradox: on the one hand, deregulated capitalism encourages techno-innovators to build increasingly intelligent and productive automatons; on the other, it blackmails workers to work faster in exchange for less and less money in an impossible race against robots. The consequence of this paradox is the precarization of work and of life more generally.

Precariousness is the general form of work relations: when work starts to be precarized in some points, the perception of precarity spreads everywhere, as competition among workers (particularly among cognitive workers) takes the place of solidarity. Every worker knows that her job can be replaced by a machine, every worker knows that his salary can be taken tomorrow by another worker. Everybody is led to sense others as potential enemies and potential threats.

Young people who work in the cultural industry know very well this precarious blackmail. Art galleries, universities, publishing enterprises, magazines and newspapers all exploit cognitive workers for free. They call it an 'internship' or something similar. Cognitive workers are lured to accept these conditions because they are investing in their chosen cultural activity the best of their personality, of their culture, of their expressivity, and so the blackmail succeeds. Doing for free what you like may be a good thing, but the problem is that one must pay rent, and pay back the bank for university loans. Ends do not meet.

The link between work and salary is loosening, but only capitalists profit from the ensuing randomness and precariousness as long as the emancipation of time from salary is grounded in the superstition of salaried work.

Convention, Superstition and Salaried Work

Because of a superstitious perception of reality, we persist in the pretence that digital production can be signified according to the old industrial paradigm.

Growth, work, salary – these are categories that have been able to explain and signify human activity in times of scarcity, within the frame of a mechanic epistemology. These categories cannot semiotize the digital proliferation and hyper-velocity that has produced abundance and excess.

Concepts such as labour, salary and growth are semiotic conventions. Conventions, however, are not only linguistic signs marking real life but are also frameworks of signification that shape our expectations and our modes of interaction. Conventions give birth to a code that has offered the possibility to access the protocols of exchange that make survival possible.

But the code based on the established conventions has since grown unable to interpret or to manage technical progress and its effects. This code is no longer working: it's unfit to rationally manage the forms of life that emerge in the digital sphere.

As production turns into semiotic recombination and exchange, labour turns into the investment of mental energy. Mental time can hardly be reduced to value, as productivity in this field is highly volatile and random. Prices turn out to be aleatory indicators of temporary *rapports de force*. Salary is finally exposed as a superstition, and is replaced more and more often by new forms of slavery, and by the sheer brutality of the *rapports de force*.

Salary is the superstition that holds together a castle that is devoid of foundations. But this superstition is ever frailer and shakier if we realize that a new wave of automation is submerging the world of production.

Should We Be Scared of the Working Android?

Google, the greatest corporation of all time, is aiming for this goal: to link operational machines with search engines that may drive those machines using the infinite resources of the network. So doing, the machine will acquire an unprecedented degree of flexibility, enabling the replacement of humans in highly complex tasks. The use of the working android is going to spread in the coming decades.

Most normal people are scared, as they think that sooner or later someone will understand that their work is useless and their job will be cancelled. They are right to think that their job is useless: most of the current jobs are superfluous as a machine can do it better, if not already today, then in the next five years or so.

In an article published by the *New York Times* on 10 June 2015, Martin Ford disclosed some impressive figures concerning technology's effect on employment in China:

> In 2014, Chinese factories accounted for about a quarter of the global ranks of industrial robots – a 54 percent increase over 2013. According to the International Federation of Robotics, it will have more installed manufacturing robots than any other country by 2017. Foxconn, which makes consumer electronics for Apple and other companies, plans to automate about 70 percent of factory work within three years, and already has a fully robotic factory in Chengdu . . .
>
> Chinese factory jobs may thus be poised to evaporate at an even faster pace than has been the case in the United States and other developed countries.
>
> Between 1995 and 2002 about 16 million factory jobs disappeared, roughly 15 percent of total Chinese manufacturing employment. This trend is poised to accelerate.[7]

In *The Automation Myth*, Matthew Yglesias denies that technology has increased productivity over the last decades.[8] Nevertheless, he admits that:

> The power of Moore's Law – which states that the power of computer chips doubles roughly every two years – is such that the next five years' worth of digital progress will involve bigger leaps in raw processor power than the previous five years. It's at least possible

that we really will have a massive leap forward in productivity some-
day soon that starts substantially reducing the amount of human
labor needed to drive the economy forward.

And he concludes:

The more likely outcome is a world with less work. And that's a
world we should welcome rather than fear.

Nevertheless, in the last thirty years the average salary of
American workers has increased by 5 percent while their
average productivity has grown around 80 percent. The
American sociologist Juliet Schor, in her book *The
Overworked American*, published in 1992, writes that over the
last twenty years of the century, the work hours of the average American have increased by the equivalent of one month
per year. 'Predictably workers are spending less time on the
basics, like sleeping and eating. Parents are devoting less
attention to their children. Stress is on the rise, partly owing
to the balancing act of reconciling the demands of work and
family life.'[6]

The trend that Juliet Schor underscored in the '90s did not
stop there. In 2013, in the book *24/7: Late Capitalism and the
End of Sleep*, Jonathan Crary writes that the average North
American adult now sleeps approximately six-and-a-half
hours a night, an erosion from eight hours a generation ago,
and down from (hard as it is to believe) ten hours in the early
twentieth century.

This fanatical self-immolation used to be a special feature
of American life, as puritanical American culture knows
little of the joys of life. But in the last thirty years this

fanaticism has been transformed into the categorical imperative of policy worldwide.

Salary

Sometimes I think that Michel Foucault omitted to write his most important book: a book on the genealogy of salaried work in classic modernity. Then, on second thought, I understand that all his books about prison and school and the panopticon and torture and bio-political domination are converging into a monumental work whose general subject is exactly this: how did it happen that human beings accepted and still endure the blackmail of salary in order to survive?

The widespread persuasion that one must lend his/her time in exchange for the right to enjoy the products of labour and of nature is not an obvious one, nor is it based on a natural necessity. Under conditions of scarcity, people are obliged to cede their time in exchange for the money necessary to buy their basic survival. But today the scarcity regime is unnecessary.

If activity was not subjected to salaried blackmail, none of this would be a problem. Technical innovation emancipates time from work, and this time can instead be dedicated to social activities that cannot be exchanged with money without losing something of their authenticity: health care, self-care, education, food preparation and affection. Technical innovation has created the possibility, but we are unable to actualize it because of the unquestionability of salary: survival in exchange for labour time.

Salary, therefore, has to be exposed as the superstition that obscures from view what is crystal clear: that work is less and less necessary for survival. The blackmail of salary turns technical innovation into a tragedy for society – when reduced to a tool for competition, knowledge becomes a cause of unemployment.

Interestingly, a free reflection on the obsolescence of the salary form is emerging in the theoretical circles of Silicon Valley. In the hub of global cognitive work, some techno-intellectuals are contemplating the idea of basic income, or existential revenue, that might dissociate useful activity from access to survival.

Sam Altman, the young president of Y Combinator, a Silicon Valley–based think tank, has interesting ideas on this subject.

'I'm fairly confident that at some point in the future, as technology continues to eliminate traditional jobs and massive new wealth gets created, we're going to see some version of [a basic income] at a national scale', Altman writes.[9] This, interestingly enough, is also the rationale used by many radical leftist thinkers to justify a universal basic income. Under one view, delightfully named 'fully automated luxury communism', humanity will overcome capitalism by having machines do most of the labor and then distributing the proceeds fairly across a public that will be able to work far less.

Existential revenue should not be considered as a provisional support for marginal people. It should be conceived of as a stimulus to be free, and therefore to offer the best of ourselves to the community.

When human work is replaced by machines, we'll finally be allowed to do what we really like.

'Do people sit around and play video games, or do they

create new things? Are people happy and fulfilled? Do people who live without the fear of not being able to eat accomplish far more and benefit society far more?'[10] This point is crucial: getting rid of the trap of working, does not mean that we will then do nothing. We will do what contemporary society needs more: care, education, affection, environmental decontamination.

In the near future, we are going to face the financial crisis and the environmental crisis, intertwined and apparently intractable.

The line of escape from these trends lies entirely in collective intelligence, in the technology that intelligent labour can develop. Capitalist greed and neoliberal conformism have brought the planet to the brink of a multifaceted apocalypse. Nevertheless, the possibility of a radical rerouting is not cancelled: this possibility is inscribed in the cooperation among cognitive workers worldwide. However, the potentialities of invention can be implemented only once the epistemological and practical limitations that comprise the superstition of capital accumulation and of salaried work are removed. These limitations produce a sort of blindness that obstructs our ability to see otherwise self-evident facts. We must emancipate human activity from the blackmail of salary: this emancipation would open the way to the re-programming of the techno-linguistic automatisms that are ruling the world at a level which is much deeper than political will.

The emancipation of knowledge from capital accumulation is the only key that may open the door out of the hell, even if at the moment we seem unable to find that key.

9

Disentanglement

Freedom is the content. Necessity is the form.

Tolstoy, *War and Peace*

Morphogenesis

Dialectical thought views history as a field of perpetual contradiction between subjects, and conceives of history as a process leading to the final affirmation of a hegemonic subject that is modelling society according to a project.

Although Marx did not explain univocally the meaning of the expression 'class struggle', the historical experience of Marxism during the twentieth century has been deployed against the background of this dialectic assumption.

In our time, however, dialectic methodology has become incapable of explaining the complexity of social evolution, and no longer provides guidance for political action.

Work and capital are still fundamental concepts, and oppositional. But they cannot be reduced to historical subjects, consistent entities fighting each other and tending to a superior order. I don't deny that dialectic methodology has been useful to describe the process of subjectivation when labour was a unified mass of people working together every day in the same place for a lifetime, but precarization has decomposed labour up to the point of dissolving the necessary conditions for class self-perception.

In order to reimagine the process of subjectivation in the context of precariousness, I would replace the dialectical vision of history with a morphogenetic description: rather than as field of confrontation between subjects, I suggest a view of the historical evolution as a sequence of entanglements and disentanglements in the process of the emergence of forms.

I borrow the word morphogenesis from biology, and I'll try to apply this concept in the field of social evolution in order to distinguish what can be defined as social speciation (the emergence of new social forms that escape the previous code) from that kind of social metamorphosis that only implies a new articulation of the old code.

Furthermore, I will distinguish between morphogenesis as a process of emergence and morphogenesis as a process of generation. Emergence is the surfacing of a concatenation that did not exist before. Generation, in contrast, is the production of forms according to a code. The process of generation is an automated process of morphogenesis, while emergence is the autonomous expression of an unprecedented form.

Knowledge can be intended as the recognition of a pattern that is coded in the present constitution of the world, but knowledge can also be intended as the creation of an original series of phenomena that do not comply with the previous code, and demand a new code by way of explanation.

The shift from possibility to actual existence implies a narrowing of the ontological field: only a narrow string of possible events will emerge from the magma of possibility that is not infinite but many dimensional.

Guattari calls this process 'chaosmosis': a provisional order emerges from the possible magma, and this order provisionally excludes other possible sets. Countless possibilities are missed because their subjective potency is not sufficient for the disentanglement of a creative morphogenesis.

In Greek, *morphé* means the unstable and changing shape that matter takes in the process of becoming, while *eidos* is the original form generating infinite possible 'shaped' objects.

Eidos is active attribution of form, while *morphé* is passive received form. 'Form', in fact, means the provisional organization of a possible concatenation of being, the (passive) effect of being shaped; this word, however, also means the (active) shaping of the environment, the process that gives shape to an object. In the history of Western philosophy, the concept of *eidos* evolved in the concept of 'idea'. When I speak of generative form, I'm not referring to the idealistic precession of the idea but the deployment of the generative information inscribed in the present. A form that generates forms can function as a gestalt; the gestalt is a cognitive frame based on the pre-selection of our perceptive reactions.

In *The Question Concerning Technology*, Heidegger writes that 'the essence of technology is by no means anything technological. Technology is a way of revealing.'

The 'cognitive frame' frames the world. The gestalt allows us to see, while simultaneously preventing the vision of anything that does not comply with the gestalt.

Gestalt and Tangle

According to the gestalt psychologists (namely Wertheimer, Koffka and Kohler), perception is shaped by the relation between perceptual stimuli that we receive from the surrounding environment and generative forms inscribed in our mind. The gestalt is enabling our vision, but simultaneously entangles our ability to see something different.

Morphogenesis is here opposed to generation: by generation I mean the process of producing objects according to a format. By morphogenesis I mean the emergence of forms that are not inscribed in the present constitution of the world.

Generation implies the subjection of the content to the potency of the existing structure. Power is the domination of the gestalt, the grid that makes invisible what exists at the state of possibility: the entangler.

In order to actualize a possibility, a disentangling potency is needed. Potency enables the subject to deploy the possibility inscribed in its composition, to organize the body without organs.

Disentanglement is the emancipation of content from the form that contains it, and the full deployment of the potencies belonging to social knowledge. Only by dissociation (not by contradiction) can different forms emerge from the magma.

Gestalt can be seen as a double bind: it simultaneously gives us the potency of seeing something, while impeding us from seeing something else. In Bateson's double bind, in fact, the context frames the message in such a way that the receiver misreads the message because of the influence of the context. Schismogenesis is the methodology that Bateson suggests to get free from the double bind, in order to refer to the self-organization that follows when content is dissociated from its entangling form, as well as to the proliferation by contagion (affective, informational, aesthetic contagion) of the new form that is generated by the schism.

In the contemporary historical condition, a question arises: is disentanglement still possible, when the mind of the social organism has been so deeply infected by the viral proliferation of double binds? And another: what is the origin of this proliferation of double binds in the social mind?

I do not see capitalism as a subjectivity, but as a gestalt whose action is structuring knowledge, labour and resources according to a semiotic gestalt.

When we look at a visual form, the present structure of our mind deciphers the visual stimulation according to gestalts that are inscribed in our mind, and it is quite difficult for us to see something other than the form that our mind is accustomed to seeing.

Wittgenstein writes that 'the limits of our language are the limits of our world'. In terms of gestalt and possibility, Wittgenstein's statement means that our language is a syntactic organization of the uncountable contents that belong to the field of our experience. From this range of possible organizations of the contents, our language selects a plan of consistency and enforces this plan so that it is linguistic organization that limits our possibilities of experience and perception.

But if language is a limit, this implies also that there are more possibilities beyond that limit. I would call disentanglement any linguistic creation that may be deemed an 'excess': poetry is the linguistic activity that exceeds the limits of our language.

Gestalt is the mental pattern that frames the incoming perceptual stimuli, turning them into form. The gestalt can act as a tangle when it blocks our ability to see things in a different frame. In order to exceed the entangling effect implicit in the gestalt, we need a poetical potency of estrangement (Viktor Sklovski calls it *ostranenie*).

Let's come now to the present social condition: the economic paradigm entangles the intrinsic dynamics of the relation between work and intelligence. Economics pretends to be a science. Actually, economists do not produce concepts for the explanation of social reality, nor express general laws concerning production and exchange. They are paid to undertake a different task: reinforcing the laws of capitalism upon the dynamics of knowledge, technology and cooperation.

Economics, in fact, rather than a science, should be viewed as a technology for the exploitation of existing resources, particularly of labour, in the unquestionable framework of growth, accumulation and profit. Economic knowledge generates a repetition of social and political procedures aimed at obtaining those goals.

Economic semiotization constrains the dynamics of invention and innovation within the limits of a system whose intent is the transformation of life into value, that is, the accumulation of capital – not good life, not pleasure, not beauty, not the pursuance of the best use of technical knowledge, not the actualization of inscribed possibilities.

We should imagine the possible political emancipation of the future essentially as an act of enunciation, a linguistic act disentangling reality from bad mathematics, the mathematics of finance.

The global debt that has since 2008 been the main concern of the political elites, has in September of 2016 grown to a size that is more than twice the size of the global economy. Over the last eight years, we have been told that the essential thing to do is repay the debt (i.e., displace common resources towards the financial system). And in order to pay the debt, we have been destroying jobs, reducing welfare, and de-financing schools and the health care system.

As a result, the debt is skyrocketing.

It is no longer a financial problem, but a semiotic one: the words that try to express the economic process have no grasp on the reality of life or technology or knowledge. The words that describe and conceptualize the economic sphere are a source of permanent misunderstanding, as they are inconsistent with the reality of human life on the planet.

10

A Short History of the General Intellect

We are approaching the end of this book, and I'm going to disclose my true intention: I did not want to write only about impotence, or about possibility. I wanted to write about knowledge.

Beyond impotence and power, beyond the fragmentation of society into a myriad of conflicting pieces, beyond the precarious fractalization of labour, knowledge is the social dimension where the bad dream of capitalism can be dispelled at last: not simply reversed, I mean wholly abandoned as an empty space, forgotten as a nightmare.

My approach to the problem of knowledge is not gnoseological, because what interests me more is the subjectivity that underlies the process of knowledge: the subjectivity of millions of minds connected worldwide, and the subjectivity of bodies who look for affection, sensuous contact and friendship. The consciousness of knowledge is the way to the emancipation of the future, but this way is obstructed by the privatization of the educational system, of research and of the entire cycle of invention.

Knowledge is not about truth, or about discovering and displaying the essential reality – it is rather about the creation of meaning and the invention of technical interfaces projecting meaningfulness into reality.

Absolute Knowledge in Hegel

The place of science and the relation between scientific knowledge and technological development has been the focus of philosophical inquiry since the beginning of the modern age. In Hegel, for the first time, the problem of scientific knowledge is linked with the problem of subjectivity. In his peculiar way, Hegel exposes his views on this subject in the preface to *Die Phänomenologie des Geistes*, translated into English with the controversial title *The Phenomenology of Mind*. [1]

> In my view everything depends on grasping and expressing the ultimate truth not as Substance but as Subject as well . . .
>
> The living substance, further, is that being which is truly subject, or, what is the same thing, is truly realized and actual (*wirklich*) solely in the process of positing itself, or in mediating with its own self its transitions from one state or position to the opposite . . .
>
> True reality is merely this process of reinstating self-identity, of reflecting into its own self in and from its other, and is not an original and primal unity as such, not an immediate unity as such. It is the process of its own becoming, the circle which presupposes its end as its purpose, and has its end for its beginning; it becomes concrete and actual only by being carried out, and by the end it involves . . .
>
> The truth is the whole. The whole, however, is merely the essential nature reaching its completeness through the process of its own

development. Of the Absolute it must be said that it is essentially a result, that only at the end is it what it is in very truth; and just in that consists its nature, which is to be actual, subject, or self-becoming, self-development.[2]

Hegel's *Phenomenology* has less to do with the 'mind' (which is why I call the English title controversial). The mind's activity (the physical brain, the historical context, cognition, communication and progress) is totally erased in Hegel. Only the process of self-deployment of something that cannot be named the mind, but only Spirit – remains. The pathway of self-realization of reason is a circle that leads back to the starting point, where the Absolute Spirit was at the beginning. 'Reason is purposive activity . . . The result is the same as the beginning solely because the beginning is purpose.'[3]

Knowledge in Hegel is a process that does not really develop anything, is never invention: it is only discovery of something that has existed since the beginning. The Absolute Being is the premise and the result of the process of knowledge, as knowledge is from the beginning the process of self-deployment of the Absolute Being.

The social process of knowledge, in its concrete manifestations, contradictions, difficulties, conundrums and misunderstanding, in its discoveries and inventions, does not exist. It is only the mediation of the self-revealing of the Absolute Spirit.

Nevertheless, in this text there is a far-reaching intuition: the process of knowledge cannot be dissociated from the historical process, and there is no other truth than the self-deployment of the subject of knowledge.

That the truth is only realized in the form of system, that substance is essentially subject, is expressed in the idea which represents the Absolute as Spirit (*Geist*) . . . Spirit is the only Reality. It is the inner being of the world, that which essentially is, and is per se; it assumes objective, determinate form, and enters into relations with itself — it is externality (otherness), and exists for self; yet, in this determination, and in its otherness, it is still one with itself — it is self-contained and self-complete, in itself and for itself at once. This self-containedness, however, is first something known by us, it is implicit in its nature (*an sich*); it is Substance spiritual. It has to become self-contained for itself, on its own account; it must be knowledge of spirit, and must be consciousness of itself as spirit. This means, it must be presented to itself as an object, but at the same time straightway annul and transcend this objective form; it must be its own object in which it finds itself reflected. So far as its spiritual content is produced by its own activity, it is only we [the thinkers] who know spirit to be for itself, to be objective to itself; but in so far as spirit knows itself to be for itself, then this self-production, the pure notion, is the sphere and element in which its objectification takes effect, and where it gets its existential form. In this way, it is in its existence aware of itself as an object in which its own self is reflected. Mind, which, when thus developed, knows itself to be mind, is science. Science is its realisation, and the kingdom it sets up for itself in its own native element.[4]

Knowledge as Work and as Emancipation from Work

The problem of knowledge is crucial in the *Grundrisse*, the lesser known text of Karl Marx that, in my opinion, is also his most important. Marx links scientific knowledge to the process of work, and particularly with the introduction of machinery.

In machinery, the appropriation of living labour by capital achieves a direct reality in this respect as well: It is, firstly, the analysis and application of mechanical and chemical laws, arising directly out of science, which enables the machine to perform the same labour as that previously performed by the worker. However, the development of machinery along this path occurs only when large industry has already reached a higher stage, and all the sciences have been pressed into the service of capital; and when, secondly, the available machinery itself already provides great capabilities. Invention then becomes a business, and the application of science to direct production itself becomes a prospect which determines and solicits it.[5]

Machines are simultaneously a tool for the appropriation and subjection of living labour, and the condition for the emancipation of society from the necessity of labour itself.

On the one hand:

The worker's activity, reduced to a mere abstraction of activity, is determined and regulated on all sides by the movement of the machinery, and not the opposite. The science which compels the inanimate limbs of the machinery, by their construction, to act purposefully, as an automaton, does not exist in the worker's consciousness, but rather acts upon him through the machine as an alien power, as the power of the machine itself.

But on the other hand:

Through this process, the amount of labour necessary for the production of a given object is indeed reduced to a minimum, but only in order to realise a maximum of labour in the maximum number of such objects. The first aspect is important, because capital here – quite unintentionally – reduces human labour, expenditure of energy, to a minimum. This will redound to the benefit of emancipated labour, and is the condition of its emancipation.[6]

The emancipation of living time from work is not a natural process, and the reduction of necessary labour time does not necessarily result in the actual liberation of living time from the capture of exploitation.

Nature builds no machines, no locomotives, railways, electric telegraphs, self-acting mules etc. These are products of human industry; natural material transformed into organs of the human will over nature, or of human participation in nature. They are organs of the human brain, created by the human hand; the power of knowledge, objectified. The development of fixed capital indicates to what degree general social knowledge has become a direct force of production, and to what degree, hence, the conditions of the process of social life itself have come under the control of the general intellect and been transformed in accordance with it. To what degree the powers of social production have been produced, not only in the form of knowledge, but also as immediate organs of social practice, of the real life process.[7]

In this enigmatic prophecy, Karl Marx outlines a short history of the future, and now is that future. In this text, the general intellect is assumed to be the actor of disentanglement. The general intellect, however, is not a ready-made actor; it is rather the field of the next struggle and of the next creation: a task for the twenty-first century, beyond the fog of neoliberalism and the miasma of the identitarian brainless body, beyond the deadly alternative that is presently suffocating the world. We live today in the age in which the enigmatic vision outlined in the *Fragment on Machines* becomes the only political map for our wonderings and our research.

A Note on the Notion of General Intellect

Why does Marx shift to English when he wants to express the concept of cooperation among mental agencies? Obviously, I don't know. Marx often shifts to non-German words (Italian, French and English). However, I would like to imagine that in this case he has a particularly strong reason.

Had he written the German words '*Allgemeine Vernunft*', one might think that he was *kokettieren* (flirting) with Hegel.

Not at all what Marx envisions. He does not care about Hegel. Marx is not dealing with the spiritual becoming-true of absolute reason: he is speaking of the social cooperation of intellectual workers who are not fulfilling a pre-inscribed design of rationality, rather combining fragments of knowledge according to different (conflicting) intellectual projects. Their intentions do not converge towards a pre-inscribed whole, they are not pursuing any *telos*. The enforced embedding of a prescriptive telos in the activity of cognitive workers is the peculiar action of power: an act of limitation, of subjection. The neoliberal reform of the educational system, that consists in privatization, is aimed at the submission of research to economic dogma.

The next fight will be about the autonomy of knowledge from the epistemological and practical hegemony of the economic paradigm.

The autonomy of knowledge is not a philosophical issue;

it is a social issue, as it is based on the concrete potency of concrete social actors: cognitive workers, workers who produce value inside the semiotic machine.

The autonomy of knowledge presupposes the independence of those who animate the general intellect.

When Marx wrote of 'general intellect', those two words in English, he was envisioning a technological environment that did not exist in his time. More than one hundred years later, we know that this environment and this universal machine is the worldwide net that enables the continuous recombination of semiotic acts (research, invention, communication) performed simultaneously by conscious and sensitive agents scattered everywhere across the Earth.

Sick at Heart

Berkeley, California. 2 December 1964. Five thousand students gathered in the campus square to listen to Mario Savio (a leader of the free speech movement) relate a conversation with the director of the university's Board of Regents.

He said the following:

The answer we received, from a well-meaning liberal, was the following: He said, 'Would you ever imagine the manager of a firm making a statement publicly in opposition to his board of directors?' That's the answer!

Well, I ask you to consider: If this is a firm, and if the board of regents are the board of directors; and if President Kerr in fact is the manager; then I'll tell you something. The faculty are a bunch of employees, and we're the raw material! But we're a bunch of raw materials that don't mean to be – have any process upon us. Don't mean to be made into any product. Don't mean . . . Don't mean to end up being bought by some clients of the University, be they the government, be they industry, be they organized labor, be they anyone! We're human beings!

There's a time when the operation of the machine becomes so odious, makes you so sick at heart, that you can't take part! You can't even passively take part! And you've got to put your bodies upon the gears and upon the wheels . . . upon the levers, upon all the apparatus, and you've got to make it stop! And you've got to indicate to the people who run it, to the people who own it, that unless you're free, the machine will be prevented from working at all![8]

Fifty years have passed since that day. The world has changed exactly in the direction that Mario Savio was then sensing as a frightening possibility.

In his words, I see an astounding anticipation of the relation between knowledge and capitalist economy, the process of subjection and privatization of University and Research, and also a sort of premonition of the destiny of the movement that, in 1964, was then dawning: the movement of students that spread everywhere around the world in the legendary year of 1968.

The first point that I want to emphasize in Savio's speech is the understanding that the university was (becoming) a firm, an economic entity whose leading principle is profit. The relation between power (military and economic) and knowledge was an important subject in the consciousness of the students, researchers and intellectuals involved in the movement of the '60s and '70s. But that relation has become absolutely crucial in the thirty years of the digital revolution.

The second point of interest in his speech is the heartsickness that Savio talks about. Knowledge, creativity, language have become labour. The brain is the main work force in the global network of digital semiosis. Simultaneously, however, the activity of the brain is disjointed from the social existence of the body. The work of the brain is subjected to the heartless rule of finance, and this subjection makes people sick at heart, in many ways.

Mario Savio and his colleagues were protesting the submission of research to the interests of the Vietnam War. Now war is proliferating at the margins of the cognitive sphere of production, and competition fuels war in every niche of daily life.

The third point that impresses me is the gesture that Savio suggests: let us put our bodies upon the gears and upon the wheels, upon the levers, upon all the apparatus, so that we make it stop. Gears, wheels, levers. This is the understanding that the movement of '68 had of the machinery of power: the old factory and the old working class was our imagination of the social conflict. It was an imagination that we drew from Chaplin movies and from the industrial landscape.

This is why we missed the point. This is why the cultural wave of '68, although it deeply changed social life in many respects, did not succeed in dismantling the machine of exploitation.

In that crowd at the main university of the Bay Area, young people were listening, participating and breathing together. Many of them have since become the animators of the process that led to the creation of the global net – Steve Jobs and Steve Wozniak were possibly there. But the movement did not understand that the most important thing was to take hold of the cognitive machine.

Because of the industrialist imagination that prevailed in the political culture of the movement, we missed the opportunity to start a long-lasting process of self-organization of the general intellect.

In the decades that followed the dispersal of the Movement, the people involved in it (flower children and militants, anarchists and Buddhists, weathermen, Black Panthers and those in similar guises) played a relevant role in the overall transformation of society: as professionals, they built the high-tech network, but as activists, they were trapped in the nineteenth-century industrialist imagination.

The only possibility of avoiding the subjection of knowledge to profit, which equals the subjection of knowledge to war, was the conjunction of the general intellect with the needs of society. But we were trapped by the old concept of political revolution.

Work Automation and Knowledge

Since 1964, the relation between cognition and automation has been a crucial issue involving knowledge and economy, technology and war.

Automation was sometimes viewed as the empowerment of the human enterprise, sometimes as the enslavement of the human soul.

In the '60s, critical thought of European origin melted with the tech-libertarian Californian culture and focused on automation as an ambiguous possibility.

Herbert Marcuse published two books that approached

the prospect of automation from two opposing although complementary points of view: *Eros and Civilisation* and *One-Dimensional Man*.

In *Eros and Civilisation*, Marcuse expressed the idea that the technical automation of work may be the condition of a process of emancipation of social life from alienation: 'A progressive reduction of labour seems to be inevitable, and for this eventuality, the system has to provide for occupation without work; it has to develop needs which transcend the market economy and may even be incompatible with it.'[9] In the same book, the philosopher emphasizes the prominent function that cognitive work was expected to have in the future of production, but also in the social movement against exploitation.

> To the degree to which organized labor operates in defense of the status quo, and to the degree to which the share of labor in the material process of production declines, intellectual skills and capabilities become social and political factors. Today, the organized refusal to cooperate of the scientists, mathematicians, technicians, industrial psychologists and public opinion pollsters may well accomplish what a strike, even a large-scale strike, can no longer accomplish but once accomplished, namely, the beginning of the reversal, the preparation of the ground for political action.[10]

Linking the emancipatory force of technology and the organized refusal of scientists and technicians, Marcuse outlines the possibility of overcoming the alienation or discontentment that Freud saw as a defining feature of civilization.

In *One-Dimensional Man*, the book that canonized Marcuse as the expression of the antiauthoritarian movement, the prospect seems different. The focus is still on the crucial function of intellectual labour, but here it is not seen as an emancipatory force but rather as a tool for domination and control.

> The capabilities (intellectual and material) of contemporary society are immeasurably greater than ever before – which means that the scope of society's domination over the individual is immeasurably greater than ever before. Our society distinguishes itself by conquering the centrifugal social forces with Technology rather than Terror, on the dual basis of an overwhelming efficiency and an increasing standard of living.[11]

Technology takes the place of terror in the organization of social control: this is why man is becoming one dimensional.

> For 'totalitarian' is not only a terroristic political coordination of society, but also a non-terroristic economic-technical coordination which operates through the manipulation of needs by vested interests. It thus precludes the emergence of an effective opposition against the whole. Not only a specific form of government or party rule makes for totalitarianism, but also a specific system of production and distribution which may well be compatible with a 'pluralism' of parties, newspapers, countervailing powers.[12]

Mobilization and exploitation of technical and scientific productivity is the condition of the new high-tech totalitarianism that Marcuse foresaw, while signalling the dilemmatic nature of automation in the architecture of knowledge and technology.

The neoliberal triumph, the annihilation of the workers'
movement – the catastrophic turn that we have been living
during the last thirty years – led to the submission of the
general intellect. This is what Marcuse predicted in
One-Dimensional Man, a book about the futurable totalitarianism based on automation rather than terror, based primarily on the subjugation of knowledge.

The Neoliberal Subjugation of Knowledge

In the second part of the twentieth century, mass education
gave a real foundation to the theoretical principle of social
mobility. The offspring of proletarians could access the
university and undertake liberal professions. This was
happening for the first time on a massive scale, and it was not
destined to last forever. In fact, at the beginning of the new
century social mobility is slowing as the average salary is less
and less capable of paying for the expenses of higher education, and the educational system has undergone a process of
privatization. Furthermore, the educational system is changing in its nature: in the spirit of neoliberal reformation, it is
no longer the space for the integration of technical skills and
humanist culture. It is being transformed into a space of
mere acquisition for specialized knowledge, a space where
individualism and competition are cultivated to the detri-
ment of solidarity and consciousness.

Here – in the neoliberal transformation of the educational process – lies the ultimate danger of the final deser-
tification of the future of humankind. If the trend towards
the separation of technical formation and critical education
goes on, by the second generation no trace of autonomous

self-consciousness will be left in the social brain, the legacy of modern culture will be reduced to vestiges for antique dealers, and the general intellect will be forever subjugated.

Mass education was not the only condition for social mobility under capitalist conditions, but it opened a way towards the emancipation of the working class: the refusal of work joined with the general intellect, and the result was a dilemmatic situation whose outcome was not predictable. The student's movement of 1968 can be viewed as the first insurrection of the general intellect: the solidarity between students and workers was not only an ideological convergence but also the alliance of two social subjects sharing a common possibility. Industrial workers were pushing towards the reduction of work time, and students were the harbingers of the intellectual potency of cognitive work, announcing the technological possibility of total emancipation from the slavery of physical labour. That alliance between the refusal of work and technological innovation paved the way to the digital revolution and the replacement of industrial labour with the info-machine. However, this process of emancipation was disrupted in the last decades of the past century, and diverted towards the financial form of semio-capitalism, as the neoliberal counter-revolution twisted the force of the general intellect against worker autonomy.

The increase in productivity, that could have paved the way to a general reduction of work time, was turned into a tool for increased exploitation. Limitations on work hours were removed and general unemployment rose as an effect of increased individual work time. The potential of the general intellect has therefore been turned against the ultimate well-being of the working population.

As cognitive labour became the main force of valorization, the economic powers tried to submit cognitarians to the ideology of merit, or meritocracy, in order to destroy the social solidarity of the intellectual force.

As it rewards intellectual primacy with money, the concept of the meritocracy acts as the Trojan horse of neoliberal ideology. Meritocracy is the hotbed of precariousness, fostering competition: when individuals are obliged to fight for survival, intellectual and technical abilities are reduced only to tools for economic confrontation. When solidarity is broken and competition becomes the rule, research and discovery are disassociated from pleasure and solidarity.

Unfortunately indeed, meritocracy is also a stimulus for ignorance.

As the evaluation of merit is acknowledged by the authority, and as the criteria of evaluation are fixed by those who have power, the learner is invited to adopt the evaluation criteria corresponding to the existing powers. Education has been the most powerful factor of social autonomy. If we accept meritocracy, we renounce the autonomy of the learning process and accept that the evaluation of our formation is wholly in another's hands.

A crucial passage in the process of the subjection of knowledge is the current dismantlement of the public education system, privatization of the university and the resulting subjugation of research to the operational rules of the financial economy. This implies the principle of epistemic primacy in economic reason that violates the autonomy of the institutions of knowledge production and transmission. The defining feature of the modern university was the autonomy of knowledge (namely its autonomy from the primacy of theology). The contemporary imposition of the economy's primacy, however, implies the cancellation of the autonomy of knowledge. Identifying the economy as universal criterion of evaluation has in fact re-established a sort of theology in the relation between learning and (economic) absolute truth.

At the end of the twentieth century, the university crisis was exposed: modern humanism proved unable to cope with the networked Infosphere. The institution of the university, as we have known it in the age of modernity, was unfit to deal with networked intelligence and the humanist legacy was in need of a reformation.

Techno-financial reason has taken charge of this reformation. Public education has been impoverished by the neoliberal ruling class: dismantled, precarized, and finally replaced with a system of market-driven recombination of fragmented skills and competences whose meaning escapes even the learner. Innovation is celebrated, but it is only allowed within the framework of the theological dogma of private profit and infinite growth.

11

Dynamics of the General Intellect

Philo Farnsworth

As long as scientific invention and technological innovation are not free of the economic epistemic tangle – as long as techno-scientific workers are obliged to look for a salary and rely on a corporation's support in order to develop their ideas, knowledge will never be autonomous.

Preserving the autonomy of knowledge is the most important issue of our time. It is the only way to overcome the corporate devastation of the world and the global identitarian civil war.

It is the horizon of possibility of our time.

During the last century, little by little, inventors have been dispossessed of the ability to know and control the function of their work of invention, and have been subjected to the rule of profit: their work has been fragmented and their formation has been modelled in such a way that they have been generally unaware of the epistemological implications of their discoveries and of the social consequences of the application of their creations.

Very few people know about Philo Farnsworth.

Very few people know about the birth of the most celebrated medium of late modern culture. Why is this so?

The reason is that the invention of the TV is the story of expropriation. The product of the inventor's work was stolen by the Radio Corporation of America, namely by David Sarnoff, its president in the decades before World War II.

I want to remember Farnsworth here because his story is a perfect metaphor for the relation between corporate greed and intellectual work.

Young Philo grew up in the Utah countryside, reading science fiction. When he grew older, he began exploring techniques for the electronic transmission of images.

One day he told his wife, Pem, that the technology he was creating would be the machine of truth, making peace possible with the ability for people to see directly what was happening in distant parts of the world. In him, the utopian side of intellectual adventure was mixed with naïve faith in capitalism and private ownership of the products of one's own work, particularly of one's own intellectual work.

In *The Last Lone Inventor,* Evan Schwartz recounts the story of Philo Farnsworth, the engineer who in the '20s invented what he called an 'image dissector', which was the basic machinery in the process of creating television technology.

According to Schwartz, Farnsworth

didn't fully realize that the process of invention itself was being transformed. Innovation became too important and too lucrative to be left in the hands of unpredictable, independent individuals. The giant corporations that had sprung up around all the new technologies of the past century wanted to control the future and avoid surprises that could topple their empires, and they were growing more and more frustrated over negotiating for patent rights with outside inventors. They decided to take on the task themselves, and in the first two decades of the new century began launching corporate research laboratories.[1]

David Sarnoff, president of the Radio Corporation of America, was aware of the potentiality of Farnsworth's invention, and made him an offer to purchase the rights to the device. Farnsworth rejected this first offer.

Then, one day, Vladimir Zworykin, an engineer at RCA, appeared at Farnsworth's laboratory under false pretences while Philo was perfecting his machine and reported back to David Sarnoff with what he learned.

The invention was then stolen and implemented by RCA. Litigation exploded, and Farnsworth was summoned by congress for an investigation into the company's violation of patent law.

Farnsworth did not trust the government any more than he trusted business. He didn't accept the idea that free competition and the dynamics of the market could result in expropriation. He did not want to seek recourse with the public authority for a problem of free competition. He trusted capitalism, alas, and he got fucked.

In September 1939, for the inauguration of the New York World's Fair, RCA displayed television screens across the city of Manhattan, and broadcast a speech by President Franklin Delano Roosevelt. Farnsworth was one of the many citizens who gathered in front of those screens.

The idea that the state guarantees the individual property of creation was first asserted in Florence in 1421. In America, Benjamin Franklin introduced the principle of intellectual rights in the Constitution. Patent law actually worked well in the nineteenth century. Since the third decade of the twentieth century, however, corporations have managed to take control of the process of invention in order to extract money from the work of scientists, and in order to subject their activity to the economic rationale.

A victim of the relation between invention and capital, Farnsworth underestimated the power of corporate-controlled innovation.

Two different skills are involved in this process of exploitation of the invention-force. The first is the complex and concrete ability of the scientist, of the technician, of the semiotic worker: ability that deploys in an infinite range of special forms of knowledge. The second is the brutal ability of the investor, helped by the accountant, the lawyer and the gunman.

Who is the winner, in the game of money? Obviously, the winner is the capitalist who knows nothing about such concrete matters as physics, chemistry, media, metallurgy, fashion or art, but knows everything about the art of the expropriation of another's work and culture. The capitalist's life has been devoted to the transformation of the infinite richness of knowledge into the infinite misery of money.

Characters

The intellectual, the merchant and the warrior have been the major characters in the fable that we call modernity. The warrior and the merchant have managed to subjugate the intellectual force to the demands of war and accumulation. In order to subjugate the intellectual function, knowledge has been fragmented and the social bearers of knowledge themselves have been fragmented as well: the multi-dimensional formation of the humanist has been replaced by the separation of the engineer from the artist and of the artist from the philosopher.

Intellectual cooperation has grown more and more technically mediated: the general intellect is functionally recombined by the networked information-machine.

Until the '60s, intellectual life was a space of exchange between the so-called 'two cultures' – techno-scientific knowledge and historic-political humanities. Then the process of specialization was pushed to the extreme, and the common ground of intellectual exchange erased. Everybody is busy working under conditions of isolation and competition: engineers and poets belong to two distant dimensions that never meet.

Nevertheless, the intellectual function is traversed by an internal conflict, whose dynamics call out to be analyzed.

I'll call the artist, the engineer, and the economist the main characters of the fable called the general intellect. Their story is the core of the social dynamics of intellectual life.

The artist, like the pure scientist, is the creator of new concepts and new precepts, disclosing new possible horizons of the social experience. The artist speaks the language of conjunction: in the artistic creation, the relation between sign and meaning is not conventionally fixed but pragmatically displaced and constantly renegotiated.

The engineer is the master of technology, the intellectual who transforms concepts into projects, and projects into algorithms. The engineer speaks the language of connection. The relation between sign and meaning is conventionally inscribed in engineering. The engineer is a producer of machines, technical combinations of algorithms and physical matter that perform in accordance with concepts.

The third figure of the contemporary general intellect is the economist, the fake scientist and real technologist whose duty is to separate the artist and the engineer, keeping them to their specialized tasks.

Economists are more priests than scientists. Their discourse aims to submit the activity of other intellectuals to the rule of economic expansion. They denounce the bad behaviour of society, urge people to repent for their debts, threaten inflation and misery as the punishment of sin, and worship the dogmas of growth, competition and profit. Their scientific conventions are not based on experience, nor in purely conceptual abstractions, but on the particular interest of the social class that is at the top of the conventional economic construction. The methodology of the economist has little to do with science: science is a form of knowledge free of dogma that aims to extrapolate general laws from the observation of empirical phenomena, drawing from this extrapolation the ability to predict something about what will happen next. But science is also able to transcend any kind of causal determinism, and to understand the types of changes that Thomas Kuhn labelled paradigm shifts. That means that scientific innovation is essentially the transgression of the established limits of knowledge.

As far as I know, economics does not correspond to such a description. Economists are obsessed with the dogmatic notions of growth, competition and gross national product, and they force social life to comply with these dogmas. Additionally, economists are incapable of inferring laws from the observation of reality, as they prefer instead that reality harmonize with their own presuppositions. As a consequence, they can predict nothing – experience has often shown us the economist's inability to predict change and contingencies. Finally, economists cannot recognize changes in the social paradigm, and they refuse to adjust their conceptual frameworks accordingly. They insist instead that reality must be changed to correspond to their own outdated criteria. Physics, chemistry, biology and astronomy conceptualize a specific field of reality, while in schools of economics and in business schools the subject of teaching and learning is a technology, a set of tools, procedures, and pragmatic protocols intended to twist social reality to serve practical purposes: profit, growth, accumulation, power. Economic reality does not exist. It is the result of a process of technical modelling, of submission and exploitation.

The theoretical discourse that supports this economic technology can be defined as ideology, a theoretical technology aimed at advancing special political and social goals. Economic ideology, like all technologies, is not self-reflexive and therefore cannot develop a theoretical self-understanding. It cannot reframe itself in relation to a paradigm shift.

The economist is the entangler of the engineer. Engineering is a technology that frames the conceptual creations of the scientist and of the artist into the technical *dispositives* for the organization of social life. In late modern times, engineering has been subjected to economic command, and the technical potencies of machines have been single-mindedly reduced to economic determination.

When the engineer is controlled by the economist, he produces machines only for the entanglement of human time and intelligence in the interest of profit maximization, capital accumulation and war.

When the engineer interfaces with the artist, his machines are intended for social usefulness and the reduction of work time.

When the engineer is controlled by the economist, his horizon is economic growth, and his activity is made compatible with the code. When he is linked to the artist, his horizon is the infinity of nature and language.

Capitalism is no longer able to semiotize and organize the social potency of cognitive productivity: economic conceptualization is too narrow for the emerging intellectual potency of a society that demands a trans-economic dimension.

The shift from the industrial to the semiotic form of production has propelled capitalism out of itself, out of its ideological self-conception, and the economic semiotization has become a tangle for the potencies of the general intellect.

The problem is the following: can knowledge truly be disentangled from the semiotic grip of the economic paradigm? Has the economist totally subjugated the engineer and captured the artist, or can the engineer get free from the economic limitations and reframe technology according to the higher intuitions of science and art – according to a shared sensibility?

12

Invention

Emancipate yourself from mental slavery.

Bob Marley, 'Redemption Song'

While we create these new worlds, we do not possess them. That which we create is mortgaged to others, and to the interests of others, to states and corporations who monopolise the means for making worlds we alone discover. We do not own what we produce – it owns us.

McKenzie Wark, *Hacker Manifesto*

No More Work

The McKinsey Global Institute recently estimated that robots could perform as much as 45 percent of all the tasks currently carried out by human workers, representing as much as $2 trillion worth of annual wages. But by making manufacturing more efficient, technology is also driving down the cost of almost every good in the world, from hamburgers to automobiles.[1]

Is Paradise at hand? Unfortunately, no, because the present gestalt seems incompatible with this possibility. The technical possibility is inconsistent with cultural expectations and particularly with the frame of semiotization that is called the economy, but is actually the hypostasis or surreptitious naturalization of the capitalist system of interpretation.

In their book *Inventing the Future*, Nick Srnicek and Alex Williams look for a way to bring about a post-work world, and describe the present workscape and the emergent tendency:

> The latest wave of automation is predicated upon algorithmic enhancements (particularly in machine learning and deep learning), rapid developments in robotics and exponential growth in computing power (the source of big data) that are coalescing into a second machine age that is transforming the range of tasks that machine can fulfil ... New pattern-recognition technology are rendering both routine and non-routine tasks subject to automation: complex communication technologies are making computers better than humans at certain skilled-knowledge tasks, and advance in robotics are rapidly making technology better at a wider variety of manual-labour tasks.[2]

That's true, but in the real world the conundrum persists, and we do not know how to emancipate the possibility (post-work society) from the present structure of the economy and from the prevailing expectations of people.

In order to actualize the possibility of unconditional basic income and full implementation of labour-saving technology, Srnicek and Williams propose rebuilding the left. In my opinion this is wishful thinking: not the political power of the left, but the social and cultural autonomy of society from capitalism is the potency that might reverse the impoverishment and disempowerment of workers worldwide.

Srnicek and Williams suggest that we should 'demand full automation, demand universal basic income, demand reduction of the work week'. But they do not explain who the recipient is of these demands.

Is there any governing volition that can attend to these requests and implement them? No, because governance has taken the place of government, and command is no longer inscribed in political decision but in the concatenation of techno-linguistic automatisms. This is why demands are pointless, and why building political parties is pointless as well.

Those who have the potency to disentangle the content of knowledge and technology are those who produce this content: the cognitarians. Disentangling their activity and their cooperation from the gestalt of accumulation is the only way.

What they need is a technical platform for autonomous cooperation of the cognitive workers of the world, towards the view of dismantling and re-programming the machine. And what they need is the consciousness of their potency.

Invention and Paradigm

In *The Structure of Scientific Revolutions*, Thomas Kuhn defines 'normal science', as 'a highly cumulative enterprise, eminently successful in its aim, the steady extension of the scope and precision of scientific knowledge.'[3] Scientific revolutions consist of the reframing of acquired knowledge into new paradigmatic frames.

Kuhn's paradigm is the basic assumption of a world-model, and the paradigm shift also implies a displacement of the point of view. Kuhn writes in fact, 'The most fundamental aspect of the incommensurability of competing paradigms . . . is that the proponents of competing paradigms practice their trades in different worlds.'[4]

The world in which the current paradigm is framed is the world of capitalist economy based on growth and salary. Scientists and inventors are forced to practice their skills inside that paradigm.

In *Grundrisse* Marx wrote:

> In machinery, the appropriation of living labour by capital achieves a direct reality in this respect as well: It is, firstly, the analysis and application of mechanical and chemical laws, arising directly out of science, which enables the machine to perform the same labour as that previously performed by the worker. However, the development of machinery along this path occurs only when large industry has already reached a higher stage, and all the sciences have been pressed into the service of capital; and when, secondly, the available machinery itself already provides great capabilities. Invention then becomes a business, and the application of science to direct production itself becomes a prospect which determines and solicits it.[5]

In the context of capitalism, invention has become a business, and the outcomes of this business are limited by the dominant form of profit-oriented economy. The word 'invention' deserves to be further investigated.

Invention does not in itself imply a paradigm shift: 'invention' is merely a technical improvement of the tools, not any change in the goals of the process itself.

Revisiting Gabriel Tarde, in his book *Puissances de l'invention* (The Powers of Invention, no English translation available), Maurizio Lazzarato writes, 'The extraordinary productivity of capitalism can only be explained by looking at the dynamics of assembled brains, not with the simple division of work.'[6]

However, in the cultural context of the French fin de siècle, the invention was also conceptualized as a living vibration. 'Invention actualises the virtualities that compose the chaotic excitement of the body of the world. Inventions . . . enable the emergence of unpredictable realities, calling them from the depths of being to the phenomenal surface.'[7]

Tarde also emphasized force-invention (not labour) as the most important factor of production: 'In Tarde the source of property is not work, but force-invention . . . The ontological status of knowledge questions the right of property.'[8] By this analysis, Lazzarato paves the way for a conception in which invention is not only improvement but paradigm shift.

Over the past century, critical theory reclaimed human autonomy from the machine. I think that this claim is no longer interesting nowadays. The machine has internalized the cognitive functions of the human brain, so the task of autonomous thinking is no longer to limit the sphere of automation but to inscribe social interests (as opposed to capitalist interests) and human goals (as opposed to technologically automated goals) in the global machine.

Automation is no longer to be seen as the enemy; automation must be analyzed from the humanist and socialist point of view.

In 1948, while working on the creation of the epistemological conditions of cybernetic technology, Norbert Wiener and

Arturo Rosenblueth presented the idea that scientists should create an autonomous space, an institutional structure in which knowledge and technology might be produced according to their own intellectual dynamics, not according to the external compulsions of the economic and military systems.

In the words of Wiener:

> We had dreamed for years of an institution of independent scientists, working together in one of these backwoods of science, not as subordinates of some great executive officer, but joined by the desire, indeed by the spiritual necessity, to understand the region as a whole, and to lend one another the strength of that understanding. We had agreed on these matters long before we had chosen the field of our joint investigations and our respective parts in them. The deciding factor in this new step was the war.[9]

Wiener's concern is that 'computers . . . might become the tools of unfeeling politicians and capitalists' and those individuals' desire to automate the social institutions over which they dominated. Over the next fifteen years, Wiener remained particularly afraid of industrial automation and even sought out union leader Walter Reuther to suggest how workers might combat the threats it posed.[10]

The Hacker and the Designer

Design is art and engineering: as an artist, the designer conceives a world for an object; as an engineer, he builds an object for the world.

As the market separates the artist from the engineer, design is turned into the subjugation of invention to the rules of the economy, that do not always comply with the rules of social usefulness.

The relation between Steve Jobs and Steve Wozniak is interesting in this context. Wozniak plays the role of the techno-skilled inventor, of the direct producer of the info-architecture, while Jobs plays the role of the overseeing designer, the visionary interface between the machine and the evolution of the human mind – that unluckily is ruled by the market.

The designer's task was rightly emphasized by Jobs, who fully understood that the penetration of technology into the bodies and minds of the social biosphere depends on the shape of the object and on the perception that users have of it. On the other hand, Wozniak embodies the hacker, the owner of highly complex skills in the field of computing and hardwiring. He remains adamant about reclaiming the social dimension of hacking, and refuses Jobs' obsession with design as merely market compliance. This difference between the two founders of Apple has marked the story of the company and the history of the net.

In an interview with the *Daily Mail* in 2014, Wozniak said:

> Steve Jobs played no role at all in any of my designs of the Apple I and Apple II computers, and printer interfaces, and serial interfaces, and floppy disks and stuff that I made to enhance the computers. He did not know technology. He wanted to be important, and the important people are always the business people. So, that's what he wanted to do. The Apple II computer, by the way, was the only successful product Apple had for its first 10 years, and it was all done, for my reasons for myself, before Steve Jobs even knew it existed. So, I had already created it, and it was just waiting for a company. And Steve Jobs was my good friend, the businessman.[11]

In Danny Boyle's film *Jobs*, the scenes depicting the conflict between Jobs and Wozniak give an interesting sense of their relationship. In the interview above, Wozniak calls Jobs 'the businessman'.

The technological knowledge belongs to Wozniak, but Jobs should not be seen simply as the person who sells his friend's product to the market. He is something more: he is a designer in the high-profile sense of the word.

Design is the creation of interfaces for social usefulness – and simultaneously it is the translation of the technological object into the language of the merchandise. The designer is the interface between the inventor and the user, but he is also the interface between technology and the economic exploitation of the products of the mind.

Design is not only the art of designing an object in such a way that people can handle it properly and easily, but the projection of an object onto the broad prospect of historical and cultural evolution.

The engineer translates the conjunctive life into connective structures.

The designer translates the connective structure into conjunctive concatenations.

The designer is the master of the invention.

Afterword: The Inconceivable

Trauma

In the second decade of the twenty-first century two different processes are operating with apparently unstoppable force: the first is a global civil war underway since 2001 and ramping up to a breathtaking pace in the year 2016; the second is the automation of cognitive activity, the penetration of AI devices into daily life and into the urban environment, paving the way to a neuro-totalitarian system.

Both processes are actually under development, both appear inevitable.

Brexit and Trump's electoral victory marked a breakpoint in the history of neoliberal globalism. In the past century, we thought democracy and socialism had defeated nationalism. Wrong. Nationalism is back, thanks to the vengeance of the white working class, humiliated by neoliberal policies and betrayed by social reformists who have played into the hands of the financial dictatorship.

This working-class revenge has unchained a wave of white racism that collides with the anger of people from colonized areas, apparent in Islamic religious fundamentalism, Duterte's style of fascism, Hindu fundamentalism and Chinese authoritarianism.

The result will be a long-lasting trauma, the effects of which cannot yet be estimated. We may witness the spread of barbarianism and violence, and the eventual breakdown of civilization to the point where what is human in the human race is obliterated. But this future has yet to be written.

The trauma will not be a mere cultural breakdown: it will possibly evolve into a neuro-morphogenesis, the emergence of new cognitive abilities.

The forms and meaning of the neuro-morphogenesis will be shaped by a therapeutic and aesthetic action. In the implications of the trauma there is the space for a culture of disentanglement for the emancipation of the inscribed possibility from the tangle of the automaton.

The way out of the global civil war fuelled by white racism and fascist resentments will only be found in a raising of consciousness among the cognitive workers of the world. This process appears unattainable today because cognitive workers lack the potential for self-organization. Impotence is the present condition of cognitive workers, entangled in the neurototalitarian process of self-construction within the automaton. The trauma will transform the relation between emotional and cognitive dimensions. The direction of this transformation is not prescribed: it is the stake of the future game.

Will the trauma disclose from the hidden folds of futurability the possibility of knowledge autonomy and of communist empathy among cognitive workers? Will the poets and the engineers find the energy to escape the salary superstition and develop the possibilities inscribed in knowledge and technology in a condition of autonomy?

Or is the trauma going to provoke a collapse of unimaginable proportions?

While I write the last pages of this book, a dark landscape is emerging, and to my perception and understanding the suicidal trends of the modern world seem unstoppable. However, what I see and what I know is far from the whole picture. What escapes my grasp, what I cannot see, what I cannot imagine, what I cannot even conceive is the means of escape.

Inevitable

In the book *The Inevitable* (2016), Kevin Kelly describes twelve technological trends that will inevitably shape the future in ways we can already perceive. According to Kelly, much of what will happen in the next thirty years is inevitable: the future will bring with it artificial intelligence, greater automation and even more screens. The twelve trends Kelly outlines will forever change the ways in which we work, learn and communicate: 'The arrival of artificial thinking accelerates all the other disruptions . . . it is the Ur-Force of the future. We can say with certainty that cognification is inevitable, because it is already here.'[1]

Although I agree with the technological content of Kelly's prediction, I don't agree with his argument that this evolution will necessarily happen in the frame of the capitalist paradigm.

I've been a reader of Kelly's since he published *Out of Control*. Biology, computation and Buddhism converged in that book: the global mind is a bio-info super-organism whose aims and procedures we cannot know and cannot resist. I enjoyed his book, but I did not fall into the conceptual trap of his bio-info Darwinism.

Darwinism is based on the idea that the fittest and the strongest will win the fight for life, and Kelly transferred this principle from the wild space of the jungle to the civilized space of the networked economy. This theory has proven right in the neoliberal age: the few individuals strong enough to exploit and plunder what is available have emerged as the winners of the late modern game. The problem is that they have almost destroyed the world. They have impoverished the working class, devastated the environment all over the planet, and pushed the majority of the new generation into the hell of precariousness, loneliness and epidemic depression. At the end of the day, the neoliberal struggle for survival has generated monsters like Trump, Farage, Orbán and Duterte.

Peace and civilization are in danger. The very conception of happiness, of pleasure, of the good life is in danger.

Now Kelly returns with his fake utopia, and declares that the future is written, willy-nilly, in the present.

Interpretation

I agree with Kelly on this point: the future does not emerge from pure fantasy nor from political will; it is inscribed in the present. Nevertheless it is not inevitable, because the present exists in the oscillation between uncountable bifurcations.

What will emerge in the future is inscribed in the present, that is true. But the traces that we can detect in the present are not prescriptions: the interpretation of what is inscribed in the present is not obvious and the evolution of the tendency is not prescribed in a deterministic way.

The interpretation of the present is the crucial point that eludes any determinist theory (like the techno-determinism of Kelly).

Rethinking interpretation, I'm led to reverse the eleventh thesis on Feuerbach. Marx writes: 'The philosophers have only interpreted the world, in various ways; the point is to change it.'

In the century after Marx, philosophers changed the world in various ways; the point now is to interpret it. The purpose of philosophy now is interpretation.

The interpretation of inscribed possibilities is the main task of philosophy in our time. We must stubbornly search for concepts and percepts which may help to develop the immanent possibility inscribed in networked knowledge.

We cannot change the world the way political revolutions have repeatedly done throughout modern history. What we can do is create concepts and aesthetic forms for the self-deployment of the possibility.

What does interpretation mean? It stems from the Latin *interpretatio:* 'explanation, exposition'.

The meaning of interpretation is to express, to bring forth what is inscribed. To translate from the language of inscribed material possibility to the language of signs and of communication.

In the living concatenation of 100 million minds, the technical possibility of the good life is inscribed. Interpreting this means organizing the platform that translates the material content of possibility into concepts that may be shared and transformed into production, exchange, and everyday life.

We must read Marx in context. In particular we have to read the eleventh thesis in context. When Marx disdained interpretation in favour of action, he had Hegel in mind. In Hegel, the task of philosophy is to interpret history in order to discover the inmost life of the Absolute Spirit. In Hegel, interpretation is an act of revelation.

Today we have nothing to reveal. It is not a problem of revelation, in fact, but of invention. Inventing concatenations and concepts able to interpret the present composition of the networked brain according to social well-being is the philosophical task of our time.

Incomputable

The relation between inscription and deployment appears inevitable only because we are unable to conceive of a different interpretation of the signs inscribed in the present. The line of escape from the inevitable is the inconceivable: what we are currently unable to conceive of, to imagine, and therefore unable to see.

Future is not prescribed but inscribed, so it must be selected and extracted through a process of interpretation. The process of interpretation of the inscribed possibilities is enabled and shaped by concepts. The dominant code (the gestalt) forbids the vision and makes what is possible inconceivable.

The inevitability that Kelly is talking about is based on the expanding process of computability. His notion of Global Mind is based on the idea that computation progressively absorbs every level of language, submitting it to automation. This theory is flawed in one crucial area: the advance of processing power will encounter its own limit in the temporal dimension (in the fleshy, mortal dimension) of human existence.

Computation is a principle of reduction and of determination. In recent decades, computation has grown to encompass a wide range of phenomena, reducing social life and human language to a determinist strategy based on a format of universal compliance. The development of artificial intelligence and the penetration of intelligent devices into the sphere of daily life and of cognitive activity imply that new areas of being will become the realm of computing. But the entire sphere of being cannot be experienced in a computer. Existence is what cannot be reduced by any amount of processing power.

The existential vibration escapes computation. Time, death, self-perception, fear, anxiety and pleasure: the incomputable is the excess in the process of cognitive automation. Therefore I assert that the incomputable is the leading force of human evolution: incomputability is why history is human.

The inconceivable is the dark side of the gigantic contemporary vibration. While the common ground of social exchange is based on computable concepts, the incomputable is turned inconceivable.

The Global Silicon Valley as Conflict and as Subject

What is inconceivable today is an approach to techno-power based on social needs rather than on economic realities. At

present cooperation among the cognitive workers in autonomy from capital accumulation is inconceivable.

Cooperation is happening already in daily exchange
among peer-to-peer producers, programmers and activists
all around the world. The project for the next twenty years is
to dismantle and reprogramme the meta-machine, creating a
common consciousness and a common technical platform
for the cognitive workers of the world.

I am a reader and a great fan of Evgeny Morozov. But I
also think that we should go beyond the critique of the
techno-media corporate system and start a project of enquiry
and self-organization for the cognitive workers who daily
produce the global semio-economy. We should focus less on
the system and more on the subjectivity that underlies the
global semio-cycle.

The worldwide, scattered sphere of production in which
different cultures and social interests conflict I call the Global
Silicon Valley (GSV).

The Global Silicon Valley has to be seen as a dynamic
sphere in which conflicts are continuously emerging, as the
deterritorialized sphere in which millions of semio-workers
are cooperating daily for the construction of the
net-automaton.

We should not see this sphere only as a homogeneous field
of abstract interactions. It is also a living web of connections
among workers who deal with different social conditions:
high-wage corporate functionaries as well as precarious
designers, engineers, artists and all the inglorious workers of
the net.

We must look at the Global Silicon Valley, the global
semio-factory, the same way Lenin regarded the Putilov

plant in 1917, the same way the Italian autonomists considered the Fiat Mirafiori factory in the '70s: as the core of the production process, as the place where the maximal level of exploitation is exerted and where the highest transformative potency can be unchained.

Although the GSV is under the control of a techno-elite that represents a small portion of the infinitely complex web of cooperation, we must create a common cultural and technological platform for the autonomy of the cognitarians of the world.

Building a common consciousness and spreading the consciousness of a possible social solidarity among neuro-workers is the task for the next decade, and the ethical awakening of millions of engineers, artists and scientists is the only chance of averting a frightening regression, whose contours we are glimpsing already.

January 2017

Notes

Introduction

1   The article appeared first in Swedish, before being published in French in *La pensée et le mouvant* in 1934. Author's translation from French.

2   Gilles Deleuze, 'On Spinoza,' deleuzelectures.blogspot.it.

3   Gilles Deleuze and Félix Guattari, *A Thousand Plateaus: Capitalism and Schizophrenia* (1987), p. 153.

4   Antonio Negri, *Subversive Spinoza* (2004), p. 1.

5   Ibid., p. 4.

6   Deleuze, 'On Spinoza'.

7   Negri, *Subversive Spinoza*, p. 70.

8   Benedict de Spinoza, *Ethics* (1883), Part III, Proposition II.

9   Witold Gombrowicz, *Cosmos: A Novel*, trans. Danuta Borchardt (2005), pp. 54–5.

10 Ignacio Matte Blanco, *The Unconscious as Infinite Sets: An Essay in Bi-logic* (1975), p. 17.

11 D.E. Cameron, 'Early Schizophrenia', *American Journal of Psychiatry* 95: 3, pp. 567–82.

1. The Age of Impotence

1   Timothy Egan, 'Giving Obama His Due', *New York Times*, 15 January 2016.
2   Paul Krugman, 'Elections Have Consequences', *New York Times*, 4 January 2016.
3   Nicholas Kristof, 'Obama's Death Sentence for Young Refugees', *New York Times*, 25 June 2016.
4   Mario Tronti, *Noi operaisti, Derive e approdi*, Roma (2010), p. 27.
5   *Zeiterlebnis*, as Eugene Minkowski puts it. *Lived Time: Phenomenological and Psychopathological Studies*, trans. by Nancy Metzel, Northwestern University Press, Evanston (1970), pp. 6–7.
6   Yves Citton, *Impuissances: Défaillances masculines et pouvoir politique de Montaigne à Stendhal*, Paris: Editions Aubier (1994), p. 27. Author's translation.
7   Ibid.
8   Stefano Mistura, *Autismo: L'umanità nascosta*, Rome: Einaudi (2006), p. xix.

2. Humanism, Misogyny and Late Modern Thought

1   Arthur Schopenhauer, *The World as Will and Representation*, trans. E.F.J. Payne (1958), p. 32.
2   Ibid., pp. 184–5.
3   Ibid., p. 273.
4   Niccolò Machiavelli, *Il principe*, XXV, my translation.
5   Ibid.
6   Nikolai Berdyaev, *Dostoevsky: An Interpretation* (1921). Author's translation.
7   Michel Houellebecq, *Les particules élémentaires* (1993), p. 76. Author's translation.
8   Kevin Kelly, *The Inevitable: Understanding the Twelve Technological Forces That Will Shape Our Future* (2016), p. 30.
9   Martin Davis, *The Universal Computer: The Road from Leibniz to Turing* (2000), p. 14.
10 Ibid., p. 1.

3. The Dark Side of Desire

1   Pope Francis, interview with Father Antonio Spadaro, 'A Big Heart Open to God', *America Magazine*, 30 September 2013.

4. Automation and Terror

1   Gilles Deleuze, 'Postscript on the Societies of Control', *October* 59 (Winter 1992), pp. 3–7.

2   Ibid.

3   Karl Marx, 'The Process of Production of Capital', draft Chapter 6 of *Capital* (1864), marxists.org.

4   Jean Baudrillard, *In the Shadow of the Silent Majorities, Or, The End of the Social* (1983).

5   Ibid., p. 21.

6   Margaret Thatcher, interview with Ronald Butt, 'Mrs Thatcher: The First Two Years', *Sunday Times*, 3 May 1981, margaretthatcher.org.

7   Interview, *Women's Own*, 31 October 1987.

8   Antonio Negri and Michael Hardt, *Empire* (2000).

9   Kevin Kelly, *Out of Control: The New Biology of Machines, Social Systems, and the Economic World* (1993), p. 33.

10 Ibid., p. 16.

11 Ibid., p. 15.

12 Bert Hölldobler and Edward Wilson, *The Superorganism: The Beauty, Elegance and Strangeness of Insect Societies* (2008), p. 7.

13 Bert Hölldobler and Edward Wilson, *The Leafcutter Ants: Civilization by Instinct* (2011), p. xvii.

14 Hölldobler and Wilson, *The Superorganism*, p. xviii.

15 Hölldobler and Wilson, *The Leafcutter Ants*, p. xviii.

16 See 'Eric Kandel, *The Age of Insight: The Quest to Understand the Unconscious in Art, Mind, and Brain, from Vienna 1900 to the Present* (2012).

5. Necro-Capitalism

1   Nicholas Kristof, 'On Guns, We're Not Even Trying', *New York Times*, 2 December 2015.

2   US Department of Defense, 'Discussion with Secretary Carter at the John F. Kennedy Jr. Forum, Harvard Institute of Politics, Cambridge, Massachusetts', 1 December 2015, defense.gov.

3   Roberto Saviano, *Gomorrah: A Personal Journey into the Violent International Empire of Naples' Organized Crime System* (2005), p. 13.

4   Tyler Durden, 'ISIS Releases "Greatest" Piece of Terrorist Video Propaganda in History, Tells US, Russia to "Bring It On"', *ZeroHedge*, 25 November 2015, zerohedge.com.

5   Wassim Bassem, 'Money, Power Draw Young Iraqis to IS', *Iraq Pulse*, 12 August 2014, al-monitor.com.

6. Money Code and Automation

1   Jean Baudrillard, 'Global Debt and Parallel Universe', trans. François Debrix, *Liberation Paris*, 15 January 1996.
2   Noam Chomsky, *Syntactic Structures* (1957); Noam Chomsky, *Aspects of the Theory of Syntax* (1975).
3   Marshall McLuhan, *Understanding Media: The Extensions of Man* (1964), p. 7.
4   Karl Marx, 'Fragment on Machines', *Grundrisse* (1973).
5   McLuhan, *Understanding Media*, p. 20.
6   Ibid.

7. Conundrum

1   Zachary Karabell, 'Learning to Love Stagnation', *Foreign Affairs* (March/April 2016), p. 49.
2   Friedrich Pollock, *The Economic and Social Consequences of Automation* (1957), p. 28.
3   Stanley Aronowitz and Jonathan Cutler, eds, *Post-Work: The Wages of Cybernation* (1998), p. 60.
4   Frank Bruni, 'Lost in America', *New York Times*, 25 August 2014.
5   Paulo Virno, *E così via, all'infinito*, Turin: Einaudi (2011).
6   Liz Alderman, 'In Europe, Fake Companies Can Have Real Benefits', *New York Times*, 29 May 2015.

8. Superstition

1   Mark Blyth, 'Global Markets Are No Longer Obeying Economic Common Sense', *Guardian*, 9 February 2016.
2   Ibid.
3   Peter Fleming, *Resisting Work: The Corporatization of Life and Its Discontents* (2014), p. 6.
4   Paul Mason, 'The End of Capitalism Has Begun', *Guardian*, 17 July 2015.
5   Richard Freeman, 'The Future of Work: Who Owns the Robot in Your Future Work Life?', *Pacific Standard*, 17 August 2015.

6   Juliet Schor, *The Overworked American: The Unexpected Decline of Leisure* (1992), p. 5.
7   Martin Ford, 'China's Troubling Robot Revolution', *New York Times*, 10 June 2015.
8   Matthew Yglesias, 'The Automation Myth: Robots Aren't Taking Your Jobs – and That's the Problem!', *Vox*, 27 July 2015.
9   Dylan Matthews, 'Why a Bunch of Silicon Valley Investors Are Suddenly Interested in Universal Basic Income', *Vox*, 28 June 2016.
10 Ibid.

10. A Short History of the General Intellect

1   G.W.F. Hegel, *The Phenomenology of Mind*, trans. J. B. Baillie (1910 [2005]).
2   Ibid., p. 81.
3   Ibid., p.16.
4   Ibid., p. 17.
5   Marx, *Grundrisse*, p. 635.
6   Ibid., p. 633.
7   Ibid., p. 636.
8   Fred Turner, *From Counterculture to Cyberculture* (2006), p. 24.
9   Herbert Marcuse, *Eros and Civilization: A Philosophical Inquiry into the Field* (1966), p. xxiii.
10 Ibid., p. xxv.
11 Herbert Marcuse, *One-Dimensional Man: Studies in the Ideology of Advanced Industrial Society* (1964), p. 7.
12 Ibid., p. 14

11. Dynamics of the General Intellect

1   Evan Schwartz, *The Last Lone Inventor* (2003), p. 6.

12. Invention

1   Karabell, 'Learning to Love Stagnation', *Foreign Affairs*, p. 48.
2   Nick Srnicek and Alex Williams, *Inventing the Future: Postcapitalism and a World Without Work* (2015).
3   Thomas Kuhn, *The Structure of Scientific Revolutions* (1996), p. 48.

4   Ibid.
5   Karl Marx, *Grundrisse* (1973), pp. 635–6.
6   Maurizio Lazzarato, *Puissances de l'invention* (2002), p. 51. Author's translation.
7   Ibid. p. 67.
8   Ibid.
9   Turner, *From Counterculture to Cyberculture*, p. 20.
10 Ibid.
11 Victoria Woollaston, '"Steve Jobs Didn't Know Technology and Just Wanted to Be Important": Steve Wozniak Claims His Business Partner Played No Role in the Design of Early Apple Devices', *Daily Mail*, 4 September 2015.

Afterword: The Inconceivable

1   Kevin Kelly, *The Inevitable: Understanding the Twelve Technological Forces That Will Shape Our Future* (2016), p. 30.